SO-AFN-946

ARE YOU A GOOD POWER PLAYER?

MOLLOY'S LIVE FOR SUCCESS

"Molloy's Live for Success promises to be the most valuable book ever written about success."
—*Cleveland Press*

"In this fascinating study of successful and unsuccessful people, personality images and body signals are examined in terms of appraising a person and setting guidelines for self-improvement. This book is excellent not only for those who want to get ahead, but also for everyone who wants to feel better about himself or herself."
—*Concise Book Reviews*

"The words 'success' and 'Molloy' are so inextricably entwined since the 'Dress for . . .' books that you almost cannot have one without the other . . . Molloy here imparts in riveting detail, from slant of shoulders to facial expression to nuance of fish knife use, the outward trappings he deems essential to the upwardly mobile executive. And the importance of it all is quite convincingly backed up by his research."
—*Savvy*

"Win at work. 'Success has more to do with perspiration than inspiration' is one of the gems in the pages of *Live for Success* by John T. (*Dress for Success*) Molloy. What makes this self-helper rise above the rest is its research. The experiences of 10,000 business men and women can't be all wrong."
—*Glamour*

MOLLOY'S LIVE FOR SUCCESS

JOHN T. MOLLOY

A PERIGORD PRESS BOOK

BANTAM BOOKS
TORONTO · NEW YORK · LONDON · SYDNEY · AUCKLAND

MOLLOY'S LIVE FOR SUCCESS

*A Bantam / Perigord Book / published in association with
William Morrow and Company, Inc.*

PRINTING HISTORY

Bantam / Perigord edition / March 1982

All rights reserved.
Copyright © 1981 by John T. Molloy.
*This book may not be reproduced in whole or in part, by
mimeograph or any other means, without permission.
For information address: Bantam Books, Inc.*

Library of Congress Cataloging in Publication Data

Molloy, John T.
  Molloy's Live for success.

  1. Success.   I. Title.   II. Title: Live for success.
HF5386.M73   1981b   650.1   81-15056
ISBN 0-553-01359-9 (pbk.)   AACR2

Published simultaneously in the United States and Canada

---

*Bantam Books are published by Bantam Books, Inc. Its trade-
mark, consisting of the words "Bantam Books" and the por-
trayal of a rooster, is Registered in U.S. Patent and Trade-
mark Office and in other countries. Marca Registrada. Bantam
Books, Inc., 666 Fifth Avenue, New York, New York 10103.*

PRINTED IN THE UNITED STATES OF AMERICA

BM   0 9 8 7 6 5 4 3 2

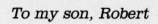

To my son, Robert

CONTENTS

	INTRODUCTION	1
1	SUCCESS AND FAILURE	5
2	SOCIOECONOMIC LEVEL	13
3	BODY SIGNALS	29
4	VERBAL PATTERNS	45
5	BEING LIKED	55
6	THE INTERVIEW GAME OR SELLING YOURSELF	67
7	SALES	87
8	COMMUNICATION	127
9	POWER	145
10	OFFICE POLITICS	171
11	THE FRIENDSHIP NETWORK	187
12	THE EXECUTIVE SPOUSE	191
13	AT TABLE	211
14	PRACTICE FOR SUCCESS	231

INTRODUCTION

This is the most important book ever written about success because it is based not on personal opinion, but on scientific research.

Nearly all books on success are founded on the ridiculous assumption that one man's personal experience or insight mirrors a newly discovered universal truth. This text, however, is based on interviews, conversations with, and observations of more than 10,000 American businessmen and women. The advice contained in this book is based on their combined experience and wisdom, not on my "omniscience."

I do not defend the premise that intimidation, craftiness, or dirty tricks are the keys to success. My research found no magic formula, no easy way. This book will not enable you to look at the world from a new angle and discover ultimate truth and easy victory. Instead, you will see the world as it is and learn to deal with it more effectively.

This book came about almost by accident. Five years ago, after my men's *Dress for Success* had been published, I had lunch with five of my friends: two successful executives from large corporations, two successful businessmen, and an attorney. They were discussing my book during the meal and complimented me on the fact that it was a useful and practical tool. When the subject switched (I don't remember exactly why or how) to the rash of success books on the market, these fellows expressed surprise at the shallowness and impracticality of the advice they gave. One said he had to let a young man in his office go because he came in and he acted like a boor. He found out later that the young man was following instructions in one of those kick-'em-in-the-teeth books. It was the general consensus that if anyone took those books seriously, their chances of getting ahead would be limited indeed.

Once they came to that conclusion, several of the fellows suggested I write an accurate book on success. I, half kidding, started to interview the five of them to see what suggestions they would give to young people. I asked them, if they were training young men and young women to succeed, what would they teach them? At the end of the meal, I had several pages of notes, most of which seemed very sensible, and I was hooked. After putting the same question to 995 additional executives, I came up with an outline for this very simple how-to book.

Almost all the men and women we interviewed agreed that success has more to do with perspiration than inspiration, more to do with energy than image. However, 98.5 percent of those interviewed also believe that successful image—including dressing correctly, moving correctly, and speaking correctly—is critical to getting ahead. They believe that a person who dresses conservatively, speaks standard English, and carries himself in an erect manner has a better chance of impressing people, and succeeding, than someone who does not. Sixty-two percent of those questioned also believe that possession of certain social skills is essential to success, and just about everyone we questioned agreed that understanding basic business strategy would be useful to any young man or woman, particularly at the beginning of his or her career.

In addition to these interviews, I applied rather sophisticated research techniques originally developed to determine the relationship of clothing to verbal and nonverbal success patterns. As a result, I made several discoveries. The first is, you're judged by almost everyone more on how to speak than on what you say. We found that men and women with poor diction and a limited vocabulary will not be trusted with an important assignment. And, while most executives were willing to admit that they would be hesitant to rely on someone who said "Toidy-toid Street and Toid Avenue," they denied that they reacted similarly to the socioeconomic level of body signals. However, our testing indicates that their reaction is exactly the same. If you walk into most executive offices with your head down if you're a woman, or your shoulders rounded if you're a man, you would be treated exactly the same way as if you had said "Toidy-toid Street."

Our research further discovered that the possession of the right visual and verbal skills is absolutely critical for advancement in most corporations and that lack of them excludes most young people from a shot at the executive ranks. The people who are being excluded are not only Joe and Jane Average, but also Joe and Jane Superior with MBA's from leading universities.

As I pointed out, we found no simple formula for success, but our research indicates that if a formula were developed, it would have to include looking, sounding, and acting like a winner. Therefore, the remainder of this book is dedicated to helping you do just that.

1

SUCCESS AND FAILURE

Although I spent most of my adult life researching image and its impact on how the world treats you, I never believed that success depended solely or primarily upon image. So I was not surprised when two research projects conducted by my company concluded that hard work, intelligence, and ability have a great deal more to do with success than does image.

Three years ago, in response to a series of questions sent to my column, I set out to identify characteristics common to successful people. In the process I learned more about failure than I did about success. I came to the conclusion, however, following interviews with sixty-two successful men and thirty-six who were failures, that failure and success are only opposite sides of the same coin. As a result, I decided to research them simultaneously and to correlate my findings.

Before I could study success and failure, I had to define them. I interviewed 300 people who represented a cross section of the American public and used their combined definition as the basis for our study. For the majority, a success is a person who has achieved his goals in life and a failure is a person whose background and ability should have enabled him to achieve certain goals but who tried and failed. This very reasonable and broad definition allowed us to exclude from the ranks of failure those who did not seek money, position, or power. Although I fully realize that it leaves a lot of people out, I think it is a fair definition.

A typical example of a failure would be a man of fifty-five with an MBA from Harvard, son of a college graduate, and of the middle class, who has been in middle management positions for the past ten years. By his own admission, his aim had been to be the chief operating officer of the company by the time he was fifty.

On the other hand, a man whose father is a policeman or a plumber, who graduated from college at night, and who works as the first man's assistant, cannot be considered a failure. In the opinion of those we interviewed, he achieved as much as could be reasonably expected from a man with his background. Although he might have wanted to be president and daydreamed about it, it wasn't a realistic goal and therefore he cannot be faulted for having failed to achieve it.

These definitions created a very difficult problem for our researchers. It's easy to identify successful people. They've achieved things. You can go to their offices and talk to them. They love to speak about their success. It is extremely difficult, however, to find people who are admitted failures. But that's exactly what we had to do. We had to find someone who not only hadn't achieved in life, but who also would admit openly that he had intended to achieve. As a result, the number of failures we questioned was relatively small.

Throughout a period of three years, I did manage to interview twenty-four men and three women who fit our agreed-upon description of failure. I also interviewed a matching group of men and women who were achievers. We didn't simply match the groups, we matched them individually where possible, one on one, on the basis of age, sex, educational background, and industry.

We started every interview with the general question, "What do you think makes a person successful?" We made the question broad so that we would not prejudice the answers. Every one of the unsuccessful people who answered said his or her life was influenced by forces beyond his or her control. Here lies the key to failure. When a person denies responsibility for the movement and direction of his life, he almost automatically fails. Failures have several clichéd explanations for not achieving. Their favorite is not knowing the right people. Of the twenty-seven failures interviewed, sixteen used a version of the phrase, "It's not what you know, it's who you know that counts." The majority talked as if having the right family connections was the key to success.

Successful men and women, however, invariably stressed hard work and intelligence as dominant factors in their achievement. Successful people did not dismiss the value of having connections. On the contrary, they usually indicated that connections were essential. But they downplayed family connections, which are an accident of birth, and spoke of making good contacts and being liked by the right people. Connections are less an accident and more a product of effort.

The second cop-out that failures fell back on was luck. Here again the difference between successes and failures was a matter of perception. Successful people believe in luck, but they invariably implied that you can effect your own luck. Winners often combine the word "luck" with "timing," giving luck an added and somewhat controllable dimension. Losers, on the other hand, talk in terms of a roulette wheel and throws of the dice.

Typical examples of failures were two men who entered the railroad industry about twenty-five years ago. Neither had prospered the way he thought he should. They claimed that they didn't advance because they joined the industry at a bad time. When I questioned two successful men who started in the same industry at the same time, they indicated that their timing and their choice of industries had been poor. They admitted that advancing in the railroad industry during the past twenty years was very difficult and they said they had to work much harder to succeed than they would have elsewhere. Both said they very much regretted joining that industry. They admitted they had made a dreadful mistake but the mistake was theirs, which brings us back once again to the essential difference between them: winners take responsibility for their actions, even their mistakes; losers do not.

Winners do something else. They work. Losers talk a good job with little or no prodding. They will tell you how hard they work and how much they do. They are more likely to tell you how tired they are and how much they have sacrificed for the company. The fact is, they don't work very hard. They tend to be clock watchers. Even if they work for themselves, they will quit at five o'clock or a few minutes ahead of time. They simply do not put in the same number of hours as successful people. And when they are working, they are usually not accomplishing much. It is partially because of their work-stopping rituals—rituals practiced as often as possible. If the coffee cart comes, they stop; if a friend shows up at their desk or calls, everything stops. Work for them is an unpleasant duty. Even the conscientious types who perform their duty take any opportunity they can to escape.

There are several reasons why people don't work. The obvious one is that they are lazy. But the reason I put at the top of my list after talking to a number of people who are failing in life is that they do not enjoy work. And it isn't just that they don't enjoy their particular job. It is a myth that if you work at something you like, you will be able to succeed. This is true only if you work hard and take realistic steps toward success. One of the biggest groups of failures in our society are people who love professions in which they are never going to get ahead—unemployed actors, painters, and singers, for example. It's not disliking a specific job that gets them in trouble. The fact is, they don't like to work at all.

Many of them won't admit it. They know not liking to work is socially unacceptable. And if you ask about their work, they'll tell you they love it. One of the tricky things about interviewing winners or losers is that clever losers are likely to give the expected winning answers. Winners can afford to be honest about not liking to do this or that, but losers have learned to offer the standard responses everyone expects of them.

One way of spotting losers is to ask them to describe the last time they got real personal joy from their work. Usually, after a long and embarrassing silence, they will recall an episode from the distant past. Winners, on the other hand, always talk about something they did last week. There is also a significant difference in the type of incident they describe. Failures almost always tell stories in which they are good guys because they helped someone else. They will tell you how Mary couldn't get her typing done and how they stayed all night to help her finish, or about Sam across the aisle who was about to lose a tremendous sale until they helped him get it. Winners, on the other hand, are not as selfless. They tend to be at the center of their own efforts to succeed. They tell about problems they solved or products they sold. They are their own heroes. They benefit most from their own labors. Losers say, "No matter how much I work, someone else gets rewarded."

Most of the people I interviewed had no idea they were failing while they were doing it. They usually discovered it too late, and discovering it too late is a convenient cop-out. Acknowledging their failure would have required action, something to correct the situation. As I was interviewing these people, my grandmother's favorite saying kept popping into my mind. "God helps those who help themselves, and God help those who don't."

In one large manufacturing firm almost everyone knew that to become a corporate officer you had to work your way up through half a dozen jobs. The length of time spent doing any one of these jobs was critical. If you were being tracked for a top position, you spent eighteen months as a line supervisor, no more, no less. Two years or more spent on the post was a sure sign you were being passed over for a top spot.

The men on the line know which executives are headed for the top and which ones are going to be around for a long time. And they treat them differently. Surprisingly, they are more generous to those who will be around for a while than to the people heading for the president's office. Yet when I interviewed one of the men who held a line job for seven years, he said that he had almost quit six months before when he discovered he was not headed for the top. That's typical of a loser. He is usually the last one to know that he is losing. Some never discover it.

Losers rarely take work home or work in places and at times not specifically designed for work. They rarely use spare time as work time. If the plane they are catching is going to be an hour late, working in the airport will never occur to them. We did a small survey of the percentage of people in first class and in coach who worked on cross-country flights. It was a very simple unscientific survey. I walked through and counted the number of people working in each section. On daytime cross-country flights, 32.6 percent of the people in first class will be working; in coach, the percentage is 12. On seven separate flights I saw more than three times the percentage of people working in first class as in coach. The relationship is obvious. Since failures do not work at home, they don't think, they don't create, and they don't solve problems at home. They hardly ever come in the next day and say, "I was sitting in the bathtub and bang, something occurred to me." That's not what they do. That's the prerogative of winners.

The most universal characteristic of failures is their lack of energy. Of the twenty-seven people we put in the failure category, twenty-four displayed markedly low energy levels. I'm not quite certain whether the low energy level is a result of failure or the cause of it. We interviewed several people in subsequent research and found that when they succeed, they become more energetic. Successful people jog, play bridge, play touch football, attend art classes, read books on success, and so on, even after a ten- to twelve-hour day. Failures, however, tend to engage in passive, nonphysical activity. They sit and watch football games on television. Unsuccessful people go home after an eight-hour day and doze in their chairs.

This book is not going to help failures, because it requires action. For those of you with guts and energy, read on.

2
SOCIOECONOMIC LEVEL

Theoretically, everyone has two socioeconomic levels, a real one and a perceived one. The main factors in evaluating your socioeconomic level are your wealth, your job, your education, and your family background. Because there is no agreed-upon formula, these factors will have various weights depending on who's doing the measuring. If you ask college professors which factor weighs most heavily, they will tell you education. If you ask businessmen or the general public, they will tell you money. If you ask men in high-status, low-paying positions such as army officers, they will tell you position. No one denies socioeconomic positioning. What is argued about is how to establish it.

In some environments, establishing socioeconomic position is easier than in others. If you are the richest, best educated, most powerful man in a small town, you will be treated with great deference. If, on the other hand, you are an unemployed high school dropout in the same town, you're likely to be treated rather shabbily. This is a simple fact of life that no one questions. In such an environment it makes absolutely no difference how well you dress, what kind of car you drive, or even how you speak or carry yourself. Everyone knows who you are, what you've accomplished, and what you have. Therefore, if you spend most of your time in a closed environment such as a small town or a small company, your real socioeconomic position will determine how people treat you.

However, if you choose to live in the broader world where most power lies and must deal with relative strangers on a regular basis as you have to in a large city or large corporation, your perceived socioeconomic level will affect the way you are treated as much, if not more, than your real one. In fact, if there is any such thing as a real socioeconomic level, only a few will be able to identify it. Not one person in ten in this larger world will know how much money you have, what your educational background is, or even what position you hold.

Obviously, there is an overlap between real and perceived socioeconomic position. It depends not only on the perception of the viewer, but also on the information you present and how that information is packaged. Everyone we interviewed agreed that a professor earning $35,000 a year has a higher social status than a plumber earning $35,000 a year, because his job tells us that he has a better education and more prestige. However, if the same plumber takes his business and expands it to $250,000 a year, most of the people we interviewed indicated that he then outranks the professor. If that same plumber goes to a party and is introduced as a plumber, while the professor is introduced as a professor, the professor will receive better treatment. But if the plumber, without increasing his income, is introduced as a plumbing contractor, which really doesn't change what he does, he may be thought to outrank the professor. Your socioeconomic position will be determined not simply by your background, your wealth, or your job, but by how you present these elements to the world.

Tolltakers in a Northeast city are a superb example of the impact of title upon position. About twenty-five years ago during labor negotiations, a union leader had their title changed from "tolltaker" to "bridge and tunnel officer." Once their title changed, he insisted at subsequent negotiations that his bridge and tunnel officers learn to use firearms; he then insisted that they be issued firearms. Finally, he pointed out very logically that they were now law officers who were carrying firearms and they should be paid as law officers. Since the police made 30 to 40 percent more, he wanted a substantial raise. Although he didn't get exactly what he wanted, he came pretty close. This union leader understood the relationship of title, image, and money.

Some people who did not understand it were librarians from Texas. When we did research on their image for the Texas Library Association, we discovered the public held them in very low esteem. More than 70 percent of those questioned believed that it was not necessary to have a college degree to work in a library and that everyone who worked in a library was a librarian. The fact is that the minimum educational requirement for a librarian is a master's degree and that most of the people you meet in libraries are simply clerks.

The problem is not one of public ignorance but of poor image. The way librarians dress and conduct themselves gives the public the impression they are glorified clerks. As a result, they are one of the most underpaid groups of people in the United States. In fact, they are paid substantially less, despite their master's degrees, than most of the tunnel and bridge officers, who are generally high school graduates. And every time there is a budget crunch, the first to feel the impact are the libraries. One of the reasons is that the people who run them announce through their poor image that libraries are not important places because they are run by unimportant people.

This is a classic example of how the perceived socioeconomic image of a group affects its real socioeconomic position. Before you join a profession or an industry, identify its perceived socioeconomic position. This perception will affect the way you will be treated and paid for the rest of your life.

I'm not contending that position is strictly a matter of

salary. I make more money as a consultant than I do as an author and more as an author than I do as a nationally syndicated columnist. Yet I find when I introduce myself to people that I get better treatment when I tell them I'm a nationally syndicated columnist than when I tell them I'm an author. And again, I am more likely to get preferential treatment if I tell them I'm an author rather than a consultant. There is no strict one-on-one correlation. However, there is generally a relationship between the perceived socioeconomic level of your job and how much you're paid to perform that job.

I first started testing socioeconomic level while researching clothing. I found that people at various socioeconomic levels wore distinctly different types of clothing and that almost everyone recognized that difference. For example, eight out of every ten American males who come from an upper-middle-class background wear beige raincoats while eight out of every ten males who come from and remain in a lower-middle-class background wear black ones. If you wear a beige raincoat people will think you're better educated, more intelligent, more articulate, more reliable, and a harder worker than if you wear a black one.

Executives, professionals, and others in high-status, high-pay positions act differently than do blue-collar workers and people in low-status, low-pay positions. When someone acts like an executive or professional, he is treated with a great deal more respect than someone who acts like a blue-collar worker. Those surveyed readily admit that most people send mixed socioeconomic messages and that very few people can be classified as solely of an upper-socioeconomic or lower-socioeconomic level. Yet enough people do fall into these categories so that characteristics of each group can be identified. If you avoid the mannerisms of lower-socioeconomic groups and emulate those of the upper-socioeconomic groups, you will receive better treatment in this world. They also agree that the mannerisms of the upper-socioeconomic group can be listed and copied.

According to our research, members of upper-socio-economic groups generally have possessions that indicate wealth and taste. They live in more expensive homes, drive more expensive cars, wear more expensive jewelry and clothing than do blue-collar workers, which facts simply announce they have more money. They also are more likely to have books and classical records in their homes, which fact indicates a certain level of taste. In addition, they will have works of art and antiques indicating both wealth and taste. Yet almost everyone agrees that simply having an expensive house and a big car doesn't make you upper-socioeconomic. They also admit it's a very good first step.

Upper-middle-class people have distinct verbal and visual signals. They tend to speak differently than blue-collar counterparts. Their choice of vocabulary is different, their accent and pronunciation is different. And they talk about different subjects. When we taped conversations of both upper- and lower-socioeconomic groups and played them back to cross sections of the public, almost everyone was able to identify the socioeconomic level of the people taking part in the conversation.

Visual signals, unsurprisingly, are as different and varied as verbal signals. Upper-middle-class people walk, stand, sit, and hold their heads at different angles than lower-middle-class people. There is also a previously unrecognized difference in the way they use and hold their facial muscles.

We accidentally discovered what has come to be known as "Molloy's Class Mask" while attempting to research the effect of eye movement on sales. We had taken video tape closeups of men and women while they were talking, hoping to show a correlation between eye movement and credibility. There was none. However, while looking at these pictures the researchers all agreed that they could, in most cases, identify the socioeconomic level of the people in the picture, even though they knew nothing about them.

When we showed these pictures to a cross section of

the public, we found that 41 percent of the people photographed gave off a socioeconomic message that everyone could identify and that more than 60 percent of them gave off messages that trained researchers could identify. At the time, I doubted that these statistics would hold true for the general public because at that stage in the research I believed that sales persons' faces are more expressive than others. This proved to be inaccurate.

To test whether everyone has an upper- or lower-socioeconomic class mask, we photographed just the faces of 500 executives, professionals, and blue-collar workers without their knowledge and showed them to 1,400 people. We told the respondents that we were testing their extrasensory perception. We asked them to guess what the person in the picture did for a living, his educational background, the type of car he drove, etc. The questions were designed to have them guess at the socioeconomic level of the person in the picture.

The number of people who guessed accurately the socioeconomic level of people under thirty was not statistically meaningful. Once a man reaches thirty, however, life seems to etch itself upon his face. Of those commenting on the pictures, 58 percent were able to identify accurately the socioeconomic level of the men in the pictures. It isn't until age forty that women are almost as easily identifiable. Irrespective of their sex, 53 percent of the photographs of men and women between the ages of forty and fifty were correctly identified by 78 percent of the people looking at the pictures. Ironically, once people reach fifty the numbers slide off again, because age, along with youth, tends to be a great equalizer. By the time a person reaches age sixty-five, the socioeconomic message in his face is as hard to spot as it was when he was under thirty. The reason the socioeconomic class mask is so important to businessmen is that when we showed the same pictures to a group of 100 executives, they picked out an amazing 83 percent of their fellow executives and professionals and eliminated the others. I can best explain this extraordinary accuracy by giving the comments they made as they went through the pictures.

"Yes, he's one of us. Yes, he's one of us. No, he's not one of us."

"He doesn't belong to the club. Yes, he belongs to the club. . . ." And so on.

What they were really doing was identifying their friends and people who looked like their friends. Obviously, carrying your facial muscles in a proper way is very important to an aspiring executive, particularly a young man who's dealing with the men at the top.

In the same way that class is not permanent in America, neither are class masks. They are products of habit. If you change your habits, you will change your look. We took twenty-five men, all of whom had been identified as lower-socioeconomic by almost everyone who looked at their video tapes, and with the guidance of an actor had them practice looking aristocratic. The technique the actor used was to have them think of themselves as judges, lawyers, or doctors, or he had them think of themselves as members of an old aristocracy, the duke of this or the prince of that. If that didn't work, he simply told them to look haughty and distant. After three two-hour meetings, most of those involved in the little class seemed to have mastered the upper-middle-class look. At least they could put it on any time they wished. As a group they promised they would attempt to maintain the look for at least three weeks. We told them we would be spying on them.

A week later we photographed them away from the controlled situation and all of the men except two had reverted to their old looks. Facial habits, apparently, are very deeply ingrained. Even if you are conscious of having a negative facial message, and you've been taught by an actor a method of turning it on and off, you will probably do it incorrectly unless you practice.

We developed a six-month program for practicing an upper-socioeconomic look. Fifteen men and three women took part. They met for one hour a week. It was a fun group; they did as much laughing as practicing. While they were away from class they attempted to maintain that look whenever possible. Several of the men bought wristwatches with alarms. When the alarms went off, the men put on the upper-middle-class look. After six months, ten of the eighteen had definitely changed their look.

A number of the men indicated that their new look had changed the way people treated them. One claimed a dramatic change. He had wanted to join a country club for some time and he knew several men who belonged. After three weeks of meeting him with his new upper-socioeconomic face, they asked him to join and they apologized to him. They said they didn't know why they hadn't asked him before. It just hadn't occurred to them. He thought he did know why.

Almost everyone we talked to agreed that the final indicator of class in America was the possession of certain social skills. Ninety-nine out of every 100 executives said that particular social skills were prerequisites to success in business and social life. They indicated that one has to have suitable table manners, know how to carry on a polite conversation, be able to introduce people without falling all over oneself, and be aware of simple rules of courtesy. Most agree that handling oneself well at a cocktail party or the dinner table is at least as important as handling oneself skillfully in a boardroom. In addition, there are social skills that some think are absolutely essential, while others think they are simply desirable. These skills consist of the ability to participate in upper-middle-class activities. Most believe you should know how to play golf and tennis. Half of them think that you should know how to sail. A few consider playing bridge essential. One mentioned hurley and another skiing, because in their social set these are absolutely essential skills. The social skills mentioned are invariably those that enable the person to participate in the activities of the rich and powerful. They enable you to belong to the right country club or yacht

Picture 1

A. Tough guy set jaw.

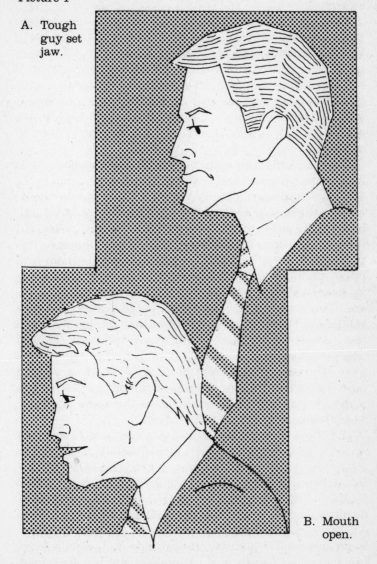

B. Mouth open.

The two most common characteristics of a
lower-middle-class face mask.

club and to socialize with people who directly or indirectly will be making key decisions about your business career.

The importance of these social skills was re-emphasized in interviews with the 100 top executives we spoke of before. All indicated that there were men with whom they had worked but would refuse to associate with socially. Every one of them admitted that socially ostracizing a man would make it more difficult, if not impossible, for him to move up in their corporation. Eighty-two said that if you can't socialize, you are not likely to succeed.

It is not only the men in the top corporations who react to upper-class and lower-class message senders. In 1973 we conducted a study with the aid of eleven client-corporations. We arranged with them to observe 312 new employees throughout a period of several years. All these young men and women had college degrees. The purpose of the first observation was to divide them into upper-middle-class message senders, mixed-middle-class message senders, and lower-middle-class message senders. There were only two lower-middle-class message senders in the first group. We eliminated them from the test. Apparently, lower-middle-class message senders don't get hired often enough to count, even when they have degrees. After three months, we made a second observation. At that time, we ascertained that 286 of the original 312 were still working in the same position. There were 184 men and 88 women.

The third observation took place five years later. We found that those we originally identified as upper-middle-class were earning $5,000-plus more than those identified as lower-middle-class. In addition, three people originally identified as mixed-lower-middle-class had now developed upper-middle-class visual and verbal patterns. All three had moved up successfully in their corporations as well. We also found that men and women from upper-socioeconomic backgrounds generally have better job ratings than the men and women of the lower-socioeconomic backgrounds. We discovered this is particularly true in those jobs in which the job ratings are more subjective. In scientific fields such as engineering and programming, a lower-middle-class background is not as much a barrier as it is in TV production, writing, and editing, the end product of which is difficult to measure.

We also found that upper-middle-class socioeconomic patterns are more important for women than they are for men. Without them, it's almost impossible for a woman to move up in most corporations. There was not one woman who changed her socioeconomic message level, and there was not one woman with a lower-socioeconomic message being groomed for a top management job. However, there were several men with lower- or mixed-socioeconomic messages still in the running for a top position.

The advantage for anyone working in corporate America to be sending off the right verbal and visual messages is obvious. The reason, however, isn't snobbery; it's sociological nepotism, more a subconscious reaction than a conscious one. I do not deny that snobbery exists, or that people are class conscious. This is a factor in most, if not all, corporations. However, there is something even more important than snobbery and that is conditioning.

In every upper-socioeconomic home I've ever been in the children have been told to sit up straight, use the correct table setting, behave themselves, and speak proper English because that is the correct or superior way of doing things. It is implied that people who do not master these social skills are inferior and that if they, the children, do not master them they will be inferior also. These admonitions are given by the most liberal parents because of their basic belief that their socioeconomic habits and patterns are superior to those of blue-collar workers. As loving parents they go to great effort to pass on upper-socioeconomic habits to their children. It is no wonder that their children, when they meet some-

one twenty, thirty, or forty years later, will be convinced
that unless that person has positive socioeconomic patterns they are lesser beings.

An experiment that demonstrated precisely this was
the report experiment. I hired an actor and an actress,
showed them films of upper- and lower-socioeconomic
body signals, and asked them to imitate them. In less
than half an hour they were accurately turning it off
and on. After they had accomplished this task, they
accompanied me to twenty business meetings.

Each time I had them with me, I gave a final research
report. Most of these reports were given to executives
from upper-middle-class backgrounds. My standard procedure is to hand out printed copies before the meetings, to go over the report a section at a time, and then
to open the floor to questions.

The young man and the young woman performed
only one task. They passed out the research reports and
sat next to me while I spoke. The only conversation they
had with the people in the room was as a result of the
basic social amenities, introductions and so on. On their
visits to the first ten corporations, they consciously imitated lower-middle-class body signals. Although they
did not use obvious lower-socioeconomic verbal patterns,
they did let an occasional lower-socioeconomic sound
slip in. They did not sound like James Cagney in a
1930s movie, they simply sounded like college graduates who came from a blue-collar background. When we
visited the second group of companies, they changed
their act. They became upper-middle-class. Here their
presentation was a reasonable imitation of upper-middle-
class men and women recently out of college.

Following the question-and-answer period at each company, I told them a little fib. I said I was thinking of
training the young man and young woman who had
left the room to deliver these reports. I explained they
were both excellent researchers, understood statistical
data, and would be able to report it accurately. I asked if
it was necessary for me to deliver the report personally

and requested their advice. Did they think these young people could do an adequate job?

Eight of the first ten were very negative. Most of the executives said that entrusting them with the report would be very foolish. Somehow they got the impression that these young people couldn't handle it and that my report would lose validity by being delivered by someone else. Among the second group of companies, the response was dramatically different. Six of the ten groups of executives said they didn't see any reason why I should have to report personally, that my time is too valuable. It seemed to them these young people could certainly do it for me. The four remaining companies who saw my assistants do an upper-middle-class act said that although they would prefer that I deliver the report personally, they would have no strong objection to the young people. In short, not one of the ten companies where the actor and actress conducted themselves in an upper-middle-class manner had anything but positive things to say about them. But eight of the ten, when they acted lower-middle-class, had nothing but negative comments. Obviously, these men would judge your competence at work by the socioeconomic message you send them. Class carries clout.

And class apparently counts heavily even if you have the right educational background. I observed 100 members of the MBA program at Harvard, Columbia, and Chicago as they went back and forth to class. I identified the program they were in by the books they carried. I may have been mistaken in 1 or 2 percent of the cases. Approximately 30 percent of the students had definite upper-middle-class body signals. The remainder had lower- or mixed-middle-class body messages. This may not seem important until I point out that of the 100 top corporate officers we observed—presidents, vice-presidents of large corporations, and presidents of moderate-sized ones, many of them graduates of these three schools—I found 96 percent had upper-middle-class body signals. In one column I wrote that I did not suggest that everyone in Harvard graduate school march to class with shoulders erect. I now withdraw that remark. I think it would be excellent advice for two thirds of the class.

Separate experiments we conducted indicated that the socioeconomic messages you give off directly affect your ability to be authoritative, to be convincing, and even to be sexy. Surprisingly, men and women who have upper-socioeconomic verbal and nonverbal patterns are more attractive to members of the other sex. We discovered this while attempting to discover if upper-socioeconomic messages made a woman more attractive to successful men and vice versa. The answer was definitely yes. Upper-socioeconomic messages make you attractive to everyone.

We used the same actor and actress we had used in the earlier research. We took them to singles bars and discotheques. They were accompanied by young college students acting as research gatherers. The male students went up to the men and asked them to judge the women in the bar on a one-to-ten basis with ten being the highest score. They were asked to judge all the women, not simply our plants. The female researcher went up to the women and asked them to evaluate the men. On the nights when our actress conducted herself in an upper-middle-class manner she rated a nine. Even more surprisingly, when the male actor carried himself in a lower-middle-class way, his score was four; when he carried himself in an upper-middle-class manner, his score was eight.

As a result of the tremendous difference in response, we asked several additional questions. First we asked them to guess the height and weight of the young man (he was five feet ten inches tall and weighed 143 pounds). When he carried himself in a lower-middle-class way, most of the women guessed him to be five feet nine inches and weigh 136 pounds. When he adopted his upper-middle-class stance, they immediately guessed his height as five feet eleven inches plus and his weight as 160 pounds. Even more interestingly, they described him as being "sheepish and ineffective" when he walked with his shoulders curved forward in a lower-middle-class way and "aggressive and masculine" when he carried himself with his shoulders and head erect.

Most of the women we questioned in the upper East Side bars were upper-middle-class. Nevertheless, the response was universal. We spoke to young ladies with Brooklyn accents and poor posture, who were obviously from blue-collar backgrounds. They were equally impressed by the young man's upper-middle-class stance as were their sisters from Wellesley and Vassar.

If you find yourself put off by the entire idea, don't be. It's actually very good news. Our research indicates that socioeconomic level in this country is not a product of background or of possessions. It is to a large degree a product of habit and perception. And since you can control the perception of others by simply changing your visual and verbal patterns and adjusting some of your social skills, you can change dramatically the way the world will react to you. You can enhance your chances of succeeding in America economically, socially, and even sexually. If you read the rest of this book and pay careful attention, there's no reason you shouldn't.

3

BODY SIGNALS

I have entitled this chapter "Body Signals" and not "Body Language" because I do not think the common term is accurate. The problem with the term "body language" is that it implies something that is not true. Body signals that I have studied in no way fit the accepted description of language. Language is usually defined as a set of verbal signals, each having a limited number of meanings affected by content, accent, emphasis, and other variables. Yet they are definite. So definite, in fact, that we have dictionaries. The problem with thinking of nonverbal communication as a language is that the elements do not have agreed-upon definitions, making a nonverbal dictionary impossible.

This misnomer has led serious researchers and not-so-serious pop-science writers astray. They have used legitimate research techniques and free-and-easy interpretation of questionable data to fit body signals into a language pattern. Their attempt to codify body signals has led them into a series of inaccuracies. The most common mistake is the notion that you can read a person's mind by reading his body language. This, of course, is ridiculous. It touches on hucksterism. Yet it is a common belief held by most laymen today. Many pop-science writers go so far as to imply that by reading someone's body language you can control him, that you can have a Svengali-like influence. They compound this idiocy by inventing the nonverbal dictionary. The most familiar entry is the folded arms definition, which states that a person whose arms are folded is signaling a break in communication. This may or may not be true. We found that just as often it means that the person is paying rapt attention or indicating that it's a bit chilly.

That definition does have, at least, some basis in reality. The researchers observed a number of people whose arms were folded and asked them what they were thinking. Their answers indicated that they were often cutting off communication. I believe that some of the research is inaccurate, but the attempt was honest. However, the people who look at research done with monkeys and superimpose their body signals on men are being ridiculous. The assumption that the society of the monkey and the sophisticated society of twentieth-century man are interchangeable is total nonsense. An obvious example disproves the monkey theory: among some of the monkeys observed, the dominant monkey proves he's dominant by staring and the submissive one admits he's subordinate by breaking eye contact. Although this can happen among men, the reverse is often true. Men who are in charge often break eye contact with subordinates as a way of cutting off conversation, ending a discussion, and imposing their will on others.

With monkeys, leaning forward in a ready-to-strike position is always a sign of mastery. With men, the opposite may be true. For example, at the end of *Godfather II* when the new leader is accepting homage from the other men in the organization, he leans back in an almost feminine stance, one that indicates that he need not physically defend himself, that he is above that. This is often the stance of men in absolute-authority positions. Only they are able to totally expose their bodies to theoretical attacks, because only they are perfectly secure. In fact, a stance that prepares a man to defend himself from physical attack is a lower-class message.

I am not for one second implying that all research on body signals is invalid. Most of the research is sophisticated, intricate, and fascinating. Although you can debate the validity of one approach or another, there is no question that some of the results are meaningful. The real problem with the research is that most of it is so sophisticated, intricate, and complicated that the results cannot be used in everyday life. Most researchers study body signals by playing back film or video tapes in slow motion. Many signals are so subtle, they are missed at real life speed, which makes the data they produce not very useful. If you spend twenty years studying the films, you'll probably have more questions than answers.

I do admit there is a limited vocabulary of nonverbal four-letter "words" and directional signals. If someone sticks his finger up in the air I know exactly what he's saying. And if someone puts up his hand in a halt motion or signals to the right or left, I again get a very simple message. But these simple signals that we all recognize hardly qualify as language.

I am not saying for one moment that you should not attempt to read body signals. With practice, you can become surprisingly accurate if you obey your instincts. You must remember that at least 70 percent of our nonverbal message sending is done with our facial muscles. Most of us are already skilled message senders and receivers. When you smile, frown, smirk, scowl, or even wink or react to others when they do, you're involved in the most sophisticated element in nonverbal communication.

Our research indicates that what most people call instinct would be described more accurately as an educated guess based on past experience. Actually, most of us are experts at reading body signals; however, we all can improve. The method we suggest includes using the new information brought about by research in combination with the instinct you've developed throughout a lifetime. Our research indicates that when you receive conflicting messages you are three or four times more likely to guess correctly if you obey your instincts. All this really means is that if you meet a man or woman with arms folded and a big friendly grin, you'd be a fool to assume you were being cut off.

We tested 162 people—100 men and 62 women—and discovered two facts: women's intuition is a myth—men guess as accurately as women do—and almost everyone can learn to read the nonverbal signals of people he deals with on a daily basis. Of those participating in these tests, 90 percent believed that the people around them gave off accurate and consistent nonverbal signals indicating mood and in some cases predicting specific actions. They all agreed that the information they gained was useful in solving everyday problems. Two men and six women told us they asked for raises when they knew their boss was in a good mood, and all except one woman received them. One man said he was now able to predict when his boss, who had a hot temper, was about to explode. He avoids him at these times. The usefulness of such an exercise was best pointed out by a woman attorney who said that many important people in her life had become predictable to a degree and, as a result, manageable.

One of the most interesting studies on body signals we did was part of a sales research project. We arranged to have video tape cameras secreted in seven different offices and tape people without their being aware of it. We had already identified the top salespeople in each office as well as the poor ones. The object of the research was to see if the good and poor salespeople had different sets of body signals. If we discovered a meaningful difference, we were going to teach the poor salespeople good body signals in hopes of increasing their sales.

We arranged to have the person in charge of each office turn the camera on during a different five minutes every day. The man in charge of the New York office apparently hadn't read our instructions and he turned the camera on for the same five minutes, sometime between ten o'clock and a quarter after, every day for three weeks. On the fourth week he was on vacation and he gave instructions to his secretary to turn the camera on. She was the only other person in the office who knew of its existence. She chose to turn the camera on between three o'clock and three-thirty every day because that was when she took her afternoon coffee break.

There was a dramatic difference in body signals from ten o'clock in the morning to three o'clock in the afternoon. In the morning, most of the subjects were erect, smiling, happy, alive, alert, and quick. In the afternoon, they were tired. Both men's and women's shoulders slumped. They held their heads slightly lower. They tended to walk and move more slowly. And while we didn't have one picture of a woman with her arms folded at ten o'clock in the morning, we had nineteen separate examples in the afternoon. We guessed at the time that this indicated that the women were more likely to fold their arms when they became tired. We confirmed this later when we were doing a similar study on store clerks and found that as the day went on, women store clerks were more likely to fold their arms.

We were also able to get women to fold their arms by simply dropping the temperature in the office a couple of degrees. It's one of the ways women keep warm. The store research uncovered several other oddities. There were three women who seemed to fold their arms all day on one day, and not on another. We found the three had one thing in common: they all had bad backs. When it rained, their backs bothered them and standing with their arms folded gave them a form of relief. Finally, we ran across a woman who walked around all the time with her arms folded. When one of our researchers asked why, she grinned a little and said when she was a young girl she was very busty. All the boys kidded her. She was so embarrassed that she started folding her arms and hunching her shoulders hoping that they wouldn't notice her bust. Although she was thirty-five and had four kids, she had never broken the habit.

So the next time you see a woman with her arms folded, you may assume that she has set up a psycho-

Picture 2

A. Male with arms folded (high on chest).
Message: defiant.

B. Woman with arms folded (low under breasts).
Message: defensive.

logical barrier and you may be correct. But you may just as easily assume that she is tired, bored, cold, has a sore back, or is busty and bashful.

We discovered that although you cannot control other people, particularly strangers, by reading their body signals, you can control the way other people will react to you if you control your own.

When we showed men pictures of women with their arms folded, the men, possibly conditioned by the current material on the subject, said the women were cutting off communication and being distant. When we showed the same pictures to women, they said that the women in the pictures were unsure of themselves, that their egos were not very strong, and that they were being defensive. When we showed men pictures of men with their arms folded, they said that they were cutting off communication and being negative. When we showed the same pictures to women, they said the men were being haughty, aloof, and more than 50 percent of them thought the men were being aggressive. Now, although there was no consistency among the four groups, there was tremendous consistency within the groups. In each group, more than 80 percent of those polled had a similar reaction, which means the science of sending body signals is far more practical than the science of reading them. If there is a Svengali effect, it's achieved by controlling the messages you send thereby controlling the way people react to you. Your body signals will determine whether you are believed, liked, admired, or thought competent. Obviously, upper-middle-class signals are a tremendous asset in business and social life.

We have been researching socioeconomic image for years. Our first research project dealt strictly with clothing. We found that if you changed people's clothing, their apparent socioeconomic level changed, the world treated them differently. When these people gave off upper-middle-class nonverbal signals, the majority of people from all backgrounds thought them more competent, intelligent, beautiful, and so on. We found the

same phenomenon takes place when you change someone's socioeconomic body signals. Men and women from
upper-socioeconomic backgrounds stand, sit, and move
differently from people from lower-socioeconomic backgrounds.

Men from an upper-socioeconomic background hold
their shoulders in an almost military fashion. While
their necks may be arched forward, their heads are
more likely to be erect. Their lower-middle-class counterparts invariably have their shoulders hunched forward and their heads down, forcing them to have a
rolling motion when they walk. Since 80 percent of all
the women in America carry their shoulders straight
and do not roll them, the angles of their head and their
neck tend to be the critical message centers. Upper-
middle-class women have their necks back and their
heads more erect.

Upper-middle-class and lower-middle-class people not
only stand and sit differently, they move differently.
Upper-middle-class people tend to have controlled, precise movements. The way they use their arms and where
their feet fall is dramatically different from lower-middle-
class people, who tend to swing their arms out rather
than hold them in closer to their bodies.

Studying these pictures will not enable you to go out
tomorrow and change your socioeconomic message. It
takes practice. There's an old joke about a young woman
who applied for a job as a cigarette girl at a fancy
nightclub. The owner, being cleverer than most large
corporations, decided to audition her. He let her have
the job for one night to see how she would do. At the
beginning of the evening she walked around with her
nose in the air, perfect posture, saying "Cigarettes and
almonds." About three hours later, her shoulders had
slumped over a little, her head wasn't in the air, and she
was going from table to table saying "Cigarettes and
ammans." Finally, at the end of the night, she was
sitting down, disheveled, yelling, "Nuts and butts." The

Picture 3

A. Upper-middle-
   class male.

B. Lower-middle-
   class male.

Key Difference: angle of head and shoulders.

C. Lower-middle-
class female.

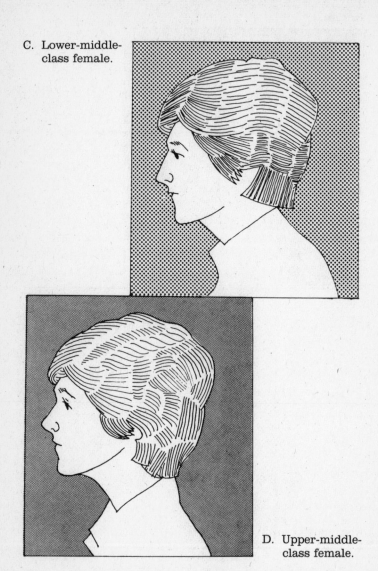

D. Upper-middle-
class female.

Critical Difference: position of chin.

Picture 4

Front view of upper- and lower-middle-class men walking.
Upper-middle-class man (left)—shoulders straight,
arms in toward body, walk almost military. Lower-
middle-class man (right)—shoulders and body roll,
arms are throwing out, hips swing.

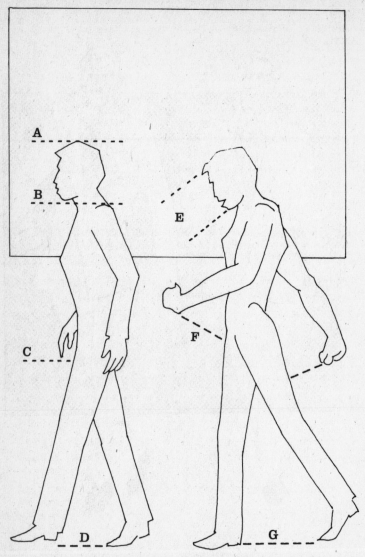

Side view of upper-middle-class stride (left): A. Head erect.
B. Shoulders straight. C. Hands cupped at side.
D. Approximately 12-inch stride. Side view of lower-middle-
class stride (right): E. Head and eyes down. F. Arms
swing. G. Long or erratic strides.

message, of course, is accurate in that in time our true character will show through.

Our studies indicate that you can chart an executive's background very accurately at the end of the day. I first noticed this when traveling with executives from various corporations. When I met them in the morning, everyone was erect and bright and executive-looking. But at the end of the day you could tell those from an upper-socioeconomic background by the way they carried themselves. They even lounged differently in the airport while waiting for planes.

All they were doing when tired was acting the way they normally acted. People under pressure often revert to past habits. Firemen in New York tell me that when they rush into a burning building, they are often greeted by a cacophony of foreign languages, that in life-or-death situations people often revert to their original verbal forms. We found that executives under pressure often do the same. We have at least two dozen examples on our tapes of men with apparent upper-middle-class visual and verbal habits who, when put under pressure at a corporate meeting, reverted to the language mannerisms of their youth. They instantly became blue-collar and, as a result, lost impact. Therefore, we must leave you with one final word of warning. If you come from a lower-socioeconomic background, even after you've mastered the upper-socioeconomic verbal and visual skills, you are going to have to control your temper and your emotions. If you explode, our research indicates you will do so in a lower-middle-class manner and, in doing so, kill your effectiveness.

Picture 5

A. Erect.

B. Controlled.

Upper-middle-class men resting at the end of the day.

C. Bent over.
Disheveled.

D. Spread out.
Uncontrolled.

Lower-middle-class men resting at the end of the day.

4

VERBAL PATTERNS

Most Americans believe that a person's verbal patterns are the best indicators of class. Actually, they are a very inaccurate way of measuring a person's past or present socioeconomic level. Geography is as likely as class to play a dominant role in developing verbal patterns. The effect is not a simple one. Upper-middle-class verbal patterns in one area of the country will test as lower-middle-class in another, and vice versa. If you have been raised in New York City or the South, your verbal image in most cases will test very poorly when you leave home. A first-generation upper-middle-class New York City accent often tests as lower-middle-class in Chicago, Los Angeles, or Detroit. In the same way, an upper-middle-class rural southern accent tests as lower-class in just about every other section of the country. On the other hand, if you were born in Boston or a few other New England towns, you have a verbal advantage when you move. A lower-class Boston accent moved to the Midwest will usually test as upper-middle-class. Ironically, the best place for an American to be born is London. We tested a London cabdriver with an eighth-grade education and everyone assumed he was a professional man and a very competent one.

The technique we used to test the socioeconomic level of language patterns is simple. We gave identical statements to hundreds of men and women throughout the country. We selected people that represented various socioeconomic levels in New York, Boston, Chicago, Atlanta, Dallas, Los Angeles, and forty-six other locations. We taped them reading statements which we then played back to the people in their communities and other parts of the country. We asked those who listened to these tapes to identify the economic and educational level of the speaker and to guess what job he was most likely to have. We found there was a significant statistical difference in the way they identified speakers from different regions. Verbal patterns were almost as important as the real socioeconomic position of the speaker.

Most strong and easily identifiable regional speech patterns tested as lower-middle-class, but there were exceptions. Being a down-home Southerner in the South is not negative. You may have a rather strong southern accent if you live in rural sections of North and South Carolina, Georgia, and Alabama and test as upper-middle-class by the professionals and the executives in that area. However, if you leave the deep South, your deep southern accent will get you into deep trouble. A similar situation exists in Texas, where there is an upper-middle-class rural speech pattern. It is as down home as the lower-middle-class speech pattern, but the choice of vocabulary and tendency to use complete sentence structure evidently make it different. Upper-middle-class rural Texans have a speech pattern that is unique to their area of the country and is, if anything, a positive influence when used by them at local business meetings. However, when the Texan leaves home he has to leave his cowboy boots and his cowboy accent on the ranch or he will be considered a rube.

The lower-socioeconomic speakers tend to display several universal characteristics. They often shorten words and chop phrases. It's called skid talking in western Pennsylvania. Blue-collar workers in every section of the country are more likely to say "goin" than "going," "comin" than "coming." They are also more likely to say "comere" than "come here," displaying a general tendency to shorten phrases by hooking words together or dropping them. In addition, the letters *d* and *t* are often interchanged as in "de" instead of "the." Generally, lower-middle-class speakers also speak less. They are simply less verbal. They answer questions with single words or even shrugs while upper-middle-class speakers, if they do not use long sentences, will more often use complete sentences or at least complete phrases when answering questions. Lower-middle-class speakers will use an entire series of words that are identified as being strictly lower-middle-class. They will say "yeah" instead of "yes," "ain't" instead of "isn't," "nah" instead of "no." Although some of these words can be found in the dictionary, they do not pass in upper-middle-class society.

While I'm sure there is nothing in this chapter to surprise any speech teacher, the difference between our findings and theirs is that they measure speech patterns against some set standard. We let the general public measure the speech patterns and found that although there wasn't any norm, there were agreed-upon local and nationwide standards. We also discovered that the people who use upper-middle-class patterns reacted more positively to others who use the same patterns. They were more likely to think of them as authority figures or experts, which indicated that reaction to upper- and lower-middle-class speech patterns is not simply a matter of snobbery, but of conditioning.

One of the more interesting findings was that people who had easily identifiable lower-middle-class speech patterns often had upper-middle-class listening patterns. These were people with a great deal of formal education but limited business or social contact. Many dentists and doctors fell into this group. They were used to hearing people speak a standard form of English on television and radio and sometimes their friends had accustomed them to hearing a better grade of English. As a result, when we played back their conversational patterns to them, many of them were upset, surprised, and dismayed. A good many determined to improve their speech patterns immediately.

I recommend that everyone reading this book purchase or borrow a tape recorder and record your normal conversations. Put it at your dinner table, in the living room, when you're discussing finances, schoolwork, or local basketball games with your wife, your husband, your children, or your friends. Play it back in the privacy of your room. You may be astounded at what you hear and decide immediate improvement is necessary.

Before you undertake to evaluate your speech you are going to need guidelines. Dr. William Formaad,[1] who heads the Verbal Communications Department of Dress for Success, Inc., has prepared a simple test to aid you in this task. It is not meant to give you a comprehensive in-depth assessment of your speech profile, which would have to be done by a qualified speech specialist. If after taking this test you decide to engage a speech teacher, we strongly suggest that you check his or her academic credentials and insist on speaking to two or three recent clients. Unfortunately, this field is filled with unqualified people. A successful career in the theater does not qualify one for this technical field. Speech improvement is not only an art, but a science. The fact that I am one of the best paid and most-sought-after speakers in the country does not qualify me to give voice and elocution lessons, and for that reason I am very grateful for Dr. Formaad's assistance.

TEST

The following sentences are geared to test common articulatory deviations and mispronunciations. Read them into a tape recorder, pausing after each sentence.

1. Dr. William Formaad, Professor and Director of Communication Sciences and Disorders at Seton Hall University, Fellow of the American Speech and Hearing Association, Past President of New Jersey Speech and Hearing Association, Elected Member of NY Academy of Sciences and Elected Member International Association of Logopedics and Phoniatrics, author of *Articulation Therapy Through Play: A Multisensory Approach.*

1. I can't understand why the plans for the animal path were abandoned at the afternoon conference.

2. Jim said that he began to get tired and quite fretful at five to ten.

3. a) She says that he is as happy as he deserves to be.
   b) Bob and Doug will see you at the World Trade Center on February the third.

4. "Snow-White and the Seven Dwarfs" is playing at
   the Radio City Music Hall.

5. Jonathan Thorpe will leave North Dakota on Thursday, the thirteenth of this month. It's his birthday.

6. Robert Lee was looking for Rory's glass on the back left seat when the red light changed to green. Then Mrs. Lee made a right turn.

7. His incredulous look made us realize that he didn't enjoy the idea of it at all. The law was being flouted; he saw it with his own eyes.

8. Singing a song or two on our way to Long Island can be amusing.

9. a) Early in the morning, Earl will boil the oil.
   b) It's been a long time since I used a pen.

In sentence 1, listen for the A sound as can't, understand, plans, animal, path, abandoned and afternoon. Do you almost hear the vowel sound in air, hair, or bear? Nasality, flatness or vowel substitution when the underlined sounds are uttered? If you live in the East your mistake will probably be nasal; in the Midwest it's likely to be flat.

In sentence 2, does tired sound like tire, five like fie, quite like kwai? Do you hear the *l* in frightful, the *m* in

Ji*m*, the *d* in sai*d*? Be sure not to slight your final sounds.

In sentence 3, do you give proper tone value (vocal fold vibration) to the underlined sounds?

In sentence 3a, does *says* sound like *cess*, *is* something like *iss* and *as* something like *ass*. . . . If they do you are "devoicing."

In sentence 3b, does *Bob* sound like a longer *Bop*? Does *Doug* sound like a longer *Duck*? Does *trade* sound like *trait*? Does the final *d* in *world* sound like a *t*? If so, you are once again guilty of devoicing.

In sentence 4, do you lisp a little? Does *Snow* sound something like *Thnow*, *Seven* something like *Theven*, *is* like *ith*, *city* like *thitty*, *music* like *muthic*? If so, you may be suffering from interdental lingual protrusion. Don't worry, it only means the tongue protrudes slightly or goes between the teeth where the s and z sounds are produced.

If *Snow* sounds like *Shnow*, *seven* like *sheven*, you are making your *s* sound like *sh*. The technical term is lateral emission lisp. Don't test this after a few drinks as you will fail.

You can test yourself with these additional sentences for the sh and zh pair and the ch and j pair:

sh—zh   It was *Sh*irley's father who was fi*sh*ing on the televi*s*ion commer*c*ial.

ch—j   Did *J*udg*e* *Ch*arles en*j*oy visiting his son's bea*ch* house?

In sentence 5, do you produce these sounds accurately? Does *Jonathan Thorpe* come out sounding something like Jona*t*an *T*orp? Do *this* and *that* sound a bit like *dis* and *dat*? Or do you favor another substitution in which case "bir*th*day" would sound like "birfday"?

In sentence 6, are you guilty of lallation? Do your *r*'s sound like *l*'s or *w*'s? Does *left* sound like *weft*? Does *glass* sound like *grass*? Does *red* sound like *wed* or *led*,

or do *red*, *wed* and *led* all sound alike? Does *turn* sound
a bit like *torn*? Speakers of English who learned English
after speaking an Oriental language may have some
difficulty in distinguishing between *l* and *r* because
speakers for whom Japanese, Chinese, or Korean is a
first language may not think of *l* and *r* as separate,
different sounds.

In sentence 7, do you put in the r sound where it is
not needed? Do you say the *idear* of it, the *lau* or *lawr*
and/or *sawr*?

Does sentence 8 indicate that you suffer from the *ng*
click? You do it when you say song and pronounce the
g. If so, this is a very difficult flaw to spot yourself.
Read this sentence to a few friends.

In sentence 9, does *early* sound like *oily*? *Earl* like *oil*?
Oil like *earl*? *Boil* like *Berle*? *Berle* like *boil*?

Does *been* sound like *ben*? Does *Ben* sound like *been*
or *bin*? Do *been* (*bin*) and *Ben* sound the same? Does
since sound like *sense*? Does *sense* sound like *since*? Do
since and *sense* sound the same? How about *pin* and
pen? Do they sound the same, or can you pronounce
them so that *pin* sounds like *in* and *pen* sounds like
men. If your *in* sounds like *en* and your *men* sounds
like *min*, you're in double twubble.

If you now believe that your voice and diction are not
what they should be, you're faced with the difficult task
of retraining yourself because both are products of
longstanding habit. Correcting them will require an
enormous effort. However, one of the factors affecting
the socioeconomic level of your speech is your choice of
vocabulary. Most of us use no more than 500 to 1,000
words when we speak. The choice of words you use is
very important. It will affect your image in a significant
manner. If you have a lower-class speaking pattern, you
will use shorter Anglo-Saxon words almost exclusively.
Although upper-middle-class speakers use these words,
they also salt their sentences with polysyllabic words
that are reserved for the active vocabulary of the upper-
middle class. For example, while a blue-collar worker

might say that a display was "flashy," the upper-middle-class speaker is likely to say "ostentatious." "Snotty" becomes "impudent" and "tough," "belligerent" and so on. If you have a limited active vocabulary, simply adding 100 to 150 words will automatically increase the perception of your educational level by three to four years and will make it far easier for you to deal with lawyers, bankers, and others of the upper-middle class.

Upper-middle-class speech patterns do not work best under all circumstances. We conducted tests on socioeconomic speech crossover. One of the most illuminating involved attorneys. We found that the active vocabulary of attorneys varied dramatically. Some used upper-middle-class words almost exclusively. These attorneys usually worked for prestige law firms and were most likely to be in corporate law. Usually, their performance before juries was absolutely horrible. We found a second group of attorneys from blue-collar backgrounds who never lost their blue-collar vocabulary. Except for technical legal terms, they stayed with the vocabulary of their youth. They were extremely effective with juries, particularly in big cities, but were ineffective when dealing with judges. The third group were verbal chameleons. They spoke one way when speaking to a judge and another way when speaking to a jury, even when they were conducting the same case in the same court at the same time. They adjusted their vocabulary and sentence structure to suit the people they were talking to. These were by far the most successful courtroom lawyers. We found the same was true of salesmen who dealt with a variety of people. Great salesmen change their speech pattern to suit the product they are selling and the people with whom they are dealing.

For some strange reason people with upper-middle-class speech patterns can, after only a few days' practice, cross over to lower-middle-class patterns on cue. The only difficulty for upper-socioeconomic speakers is in mimicking lower-class speech rhythms. Moving a speaker in the other direction takes months.

There is a tricky difference in rhythm between upper-socioeconomic and lower-socioeconomic speech. Upper-socioeconomic speech tends to be softer, easier, and broken into neater patterns. Lower-socioeconomic speech patterns tend to be jumpy and hesitating. In the same way that upper-socioeconomic people are used to answering in complete sentences, they are also conditioned to having people speak to them in the same fashion. If someone gives them a very short answer, they are not ready to respond and find the silence uncomfortable. The opposite reaction takes place when upper-middle-class people speak to lower-middle-class people. Lower-middle-class listeners are always irritated at their inability to say something because upper-middle-class speakers seem to be going on forever. Each group is annoyed by the vocal patterns of the other.

If you have to deal across socioeconomic lines, you must start listening very carefully to how members of the other group speak. If you are from a lower-middle-class background, you must be patient. Wait until people are finished and don't be annoyed by it. Realize it's a normal speech pattern. If you are from an upper-middle-class background, you have to pay careful attention, particularly to eye movement, which indicates that lower-middle-class people have finished their statement and expect an immediate response. However, although this is a critical part of the speech patterning, I do suggest that you not try it on your own or with a traditional speech teacher. You would probably be better off with an acting coach. And it will take a lifetime. As I said in the introduction, there is no easy way.

5

BEING LIKED

Bill stuck his head into my office and said, "Is this the place they're hiring researchers?" His hair was disheveled and he had an annoying silly grin on his face and I was tempted to say, no. But I said yes because at the time I was desperately looking for a project chief.

I had just received a research contract from a good client, had already hired fifteen professors who were themselves in the process of hiring students, and I needed someone to oversee the project. When I got to talking to this sloppy fellow, I found he was ideally qualified: master's degree in statistics, research background, experience in a clothing store. He was like a dream come true. The only problem with the dream was that I really didn't want to hire him. I put off hiring him until the next day, even though by any logical standard I should have taken him on then and there.

The job started two days later and I was called out of town unexpectedly and didn't get a chance to oversee it the way I wanted to. When I returned, to my delight and surprise the project had been completed. Bill had done a magnificent job. He had adjusted the data-gathering methods to suit the situation without my holding his hand. He had fired one professor who was not doing his job and hired another one who did. There was no question about it, the man was a first-class project chief. As a result, he became a semipermanent part of my organization.

When I discovered three months later that he had taken a job teaching in a local university, I was delighted. It enabled me to hire him on a regular basis and from that point on I did. But I must admit, I never liked him. I only hired him to work at a distance. I attempted to stay away from projects that he ran. I did not become involved with him personally for almost two years.

A client offered me a nice fat research contract, a cost-plus deal with a built-in bonus for results. They wanted me to put together a research team and to identify something that had never been researched before. The problem was that we had no method of going about it and, frankly, didn't know whether it could be done.

When my company runs across a new problem, we have a standard procedure for attacking it. We bring together our most experienced people, throw the problem on the table, and hope that they can, among them, come up with a solution. This project required two meetings. Bill was present at both. Unfortunately, the meetings were unproductive. I walked away thinking that my beautiful six-figure research contract was going to slide through my fingers because I couldn't figure out a way to do it, and yet I knew it could be done.

One of my best people was out of town and had to miss the meetings. He requested that I tape them, and when he returned I played them for him. Ten minutes into the first tape Bill made a suggestion that seemed to both of us to solve the problem. When I first heard his suggestion I guessed that I wasn't listening, but I wondered why everyone else had missed it. We let the tape run, mostly because we were sitting there eating sandwiches, when to my surprise, I heard Bill repeat his suggestion twice more. When we played the second tape, we found that he repeated the suggestion again. I was astonished and embarrassed that I had sat in on two meetings looking for a solution to a problem and ignored it when it was given to me. I instinctively recognized the reason. No one listened to Bill because no one really liked him. And I looked upon it as a personal flaw and made up my mind to listen to him in the future.

Our organization expanded during the next few years and we became more sophisticated and a little bit more affluent. We still held the same meetings but when someone couldn't make one, we video taped the important discussions. It was only after watching a couple of these video tapes that I realized why no one listened to Bill. No one looked at him when he talked, he annoyed people. If you listened to him, what he said didn't bother you. But if you watched him while he talked, it was very disturbing. His facial expressions often didn't match what he was saying. At times he would be animated when he should be bland, and at other times he would be bland when he should be animated. It seemed obvious he didn't know what he was doing. With a grin on his face, he made a comment about having to let half a dozen people go. The look was almost satanic in context, and yet I know he worked very hard to get another commission so that those people could continue to work. Obviously, he was sending out inaccurate messages. When he meant to say one thing, he actually said another to everyone and as a result turned them off.

He also had jerky, unsure movements. He pushed papers out on the table before they were expected or after they were needed. When he passed papers he shoved them at people rather than handing them to them. He seemed almost rude. In addition, when others were speaking he moved in his chair, looked away, rolled his eyes, fidgeted, and generally gave off the message that he was bored or inattentive when in actual fact, I could tell from his work that he was neither. His movements surprised the three of us who looked at them and tried to analyze them. They were completely unpredictable. We never discussed our findings with him because we didn't think there was any point. However, I realized that his inability to communicate accurately made him less useful to the organization and I avoided using him on jobs requiring public contact.

A couple of years later, I had a major project going in the Northeast. The contract had a built-in penalty clause tied to a time element. If we didn't finish in time, we not only wouldn't make money, we also could lose quite a bit. As things usually happen in those cases, a major snowstorm occurred just as we were completing the project. I gave up on the idea of finishing on time and went home. Bill, however, was as good a project manager as he'd ever been. He borrowed a four-wheel-drive vehicle, drove all day and all night picking up data forms from three states, brought them back, slept a couple of hours, and stayed up for twenty-four hours to finish the project. When I found out what he'd done, I was very grateful. He'd saved me a lot of money and I said to him, "If there is anything I can do for you, Bill, I will." And then it occurred to me that there was something I could do.

I told him that I was trying to do him a favor but he probably wouldn't like me when I finished. I was going to show him some tapes of himself because he had a problem. I played the audio tapes of that first meeting and then the follow-up video tapes and explained to him in detail what he was doing. To my delight and surprise he reacted fairly positively to the information. He asked me if he could use the company facilities to research himself. Of course, I said yes.

As a researcher, he started very logically. He researched his voice because we had developed proven methods for doing that. For years we had been helping politicians develop high-authority voices to match their high-authority message. His testing indicated that he had the same problem as most politicians. He tested as far more credible when he dropped his voice by a full octave. He brought it down almost overnight. He then set up a standard five-member research team and called a meeting during which he ran the video tapes. All the members, once they knew what they were looking for, immediately noticed the mismatched message system. Although he was one of the most professional researchers I have ever met and was fully aware that he needed an independent research team's reaction to test accurately, I think he regretted that we were there when he played the tapes, because as he played them he kept mumbling to himself, "My God, am I really doing that?" But he quickly settled down, started making notes, and wrote one of the finest research reports I have ever read.

I closed up the office that night and went home. At about eight o'clock I received a call from him. He seemed upset and I thought he finally had been embarrassed by the whole thing. But it wasn't that at all. When he had sat down with his wife and four sons to have dinner that night, he realized that two of his sons were sending off the same type of mismatched messages that he was. After talking to them for a few minutes, he discovered that they, as he had been, were very unpopular in school. They didn't have many friends, they found it difficult to make new friends and found it difficult to express themselves in a group. Life for them was as unpleasant as it had been for him. (He told me later he never felt so guilty about anything in his entire life. He knew how unpleasant it could be for a person who was disliked by almost everyone.)

He asked me if I would come over that night with copies of his video tapes and a recorder. He wanted to show them to his boys and explain to them that being unpopular was not part of their character, it was something he had taught them. He wanted me there to back him up and help him explain the difference to his sons.

Naturally, I went over right away. Although it was difficult to show the difference between message-sending systems to amateurs, particularly young boys who were used to their father's message system, we finally succeeded. They began to see that their father's and their message-sending systems were not what everyone expected. Once we had identified the problem we were halfway to a solution.

After I discussed it with Bill and the boys we decided to work together to correct their message systems. Our first job would be to identify the mistakes they were making. This turned out to be more difficult than we had thought, since the minute we turned on a video camera that night everyone started acting and sending artificial messages. We agreed we would have to video tape them over a long period of time so that they could become used to the camera and ignore it. They promised to eat dinner every night at the dining room table: the three family members with the broken message systems sitting at one end of the table and the camera at the other. The camera would run during every meal. We assumed that during the first couple of meals they would be uptight and acting and their message systems would be off, but we also believed, and we proved to be right, that they would eventually get used to the camera and forget about it and resume their normal message patterns.

I thought at the time that changing these message systems would be a very complicated procedure that would take many months, if not years. Happily, I was mistaken.

The cure didn't take nearly as long as we had thought. The minute the boys were aware of the fact that they were sending off mixed messages, they stopped doing it. Half of it stopped immediately. They began to correct themselves. One boy started carrying on animated conversations before a mirror. We found that he learned more quickly than the others. We asked both Bill and his other son to do this. It turned out to be an excellent technique.

If you have mixed-message-sending systems, get yourself a full-length mirror and talk to it and pretend that the mirror is carrying on the other end of the conversation. You will correct part of your negative message system within a week or two. It's a very simple procedure and it works almost every time. It worked not only with Bill and the boys, but also with many others.

The results were just spectacular. Bill reported that he was being treated the way he always dreamed of being treated. He stopped working for us several months later because he received two promotions at the university. He said that for the first time in his life people listened to him and promoted him.

He was even happier about his sons. One of the boys said that for the first time he got along with girls. He was fifteen or sixteen and for him this was very important. The other one, who was only twelve, said that for the first time in his life he was happy. When we first talked to him, he said that he thought that nobody in the world liked him, he wasn't going to like anybody, that everybody was his enemy and that they all could go to hell. To think that way when you're twelve must be terrible. He no longer thinks that way because his world changed.

Bill's story is very important because Bill does not represent a small minority. Approximately 10 to 15 percent of the population send off negative mixed verbal-visual messages. In addition to sending them, they teach them to their children.

We went to three rural school districts where parents and grandparents had attended the same schools as their children. We borrowed a series of class pictures taken eighteen to twenty-five years apart. These were pictures of the fathers and grandfathers of the children presently in school. We went out in the community and asked former classmates to identify those who were popular and those who were unpopular. We discovered that the men who were popular had popular sons and the men who were unpopular had unpopular sons. The correlation was not as high with women, but there definitely was one. Many of these youngsters were sending off the same mixed verbal-visual messages as their parents. If you have an unpopular message system, you are probably teaching this to your children.

As I pointed out earlier, it is a very simple flaw to correct and you can make the correction at almost any point in your life. We've had men and women in their late sixties who were sending out incorrect message systems and changed them with a little practice. It's not difficult at all. The minute you realize you're doing it, you're three quarters of the way toward cure.

You don't have to hire anyone, you don't have to go to a clinic. All you usually have to do is buy a big mirror and practice. It will take about six months for most who use this method to change their message system.

I personally consider this research project the most important I ever completed—not only because it helps people succeed, but for the first time I think I have helped people cope. There is nothing more delightful than working with men or women who have been unpopular and unhappy all their lives if after a few hours you can really help them. It is particularly delightful when they go from being unpopular to very popular, and many of them do. Because of their handicap, they had learned to compensate. They were often clever, witty, and friendly. When they started sending accurate messages, people began to like them.

Sending incorrect messages can be a fatal career flaw. You can neither convince nor command if you are sending off mixed messages. Of the 260 successful male and female executives we tested, not one was a mixed message sender. Obviously, poor message senders do not become successful executives.

And it is just as obvious that people who send off mismatched messages would make very poor salesmen. You would think they would avoid the field of sales, but you're wrong. There's a higher percentage of people with negative message systems in sales than there is among the general population. To make it even more difficult, salesmen tend to be blind to this particular fault. The reason for this blind spot is that being liked is so critical to their success, they hate to admit to failure in that area. I also believe that many people go into sales to prove that they're likable when they're not. It's ironic, therefore, that sales attracts people who can never sell. We have identified men who have been in sales for twenty to twenty-five years and were never anything but third-rate order takers because of this mixed visual-verbal message system. We turned 50 percent of them into salesmen in a matter of a couple of weeks by giving them a very small set of instructions and a large mirror.

One salesman came to us denying that he gave off visual-verbal mixed messages, even though our test showed clearly that he did. When we showed him his video tapes and taught him how to correct his message-sending system, his sales improved so dramatically that he turned his life around. After six weeks, he went from the bottom of his sales force to the sales honor list in his company. At the end of six months, he was one of the three leading salesmen in the company.

Therefore, I am going to suggest to everyone, particularly salesmen, conduct a simple test on themselves. First ask yourself, am I one of these unpopular people? You probably know whether you are or not. If you are not sure, mixed-message senders are very easy to identify. In every office and classroom there are one or two people who are not part of the group. They have been ostracized not because they are stinkers—some of the biggest stinkers we know are charming and we like being around them even though we may not trust them— but because they rubbed us and rubbed other people the wrong way. If you have been left out, you are probably a negative message sender.

We suggest you get your hands on a video recorder and record. The success rate with the video tape is 80 percent. You must become so used to the camera that you ignore it. You can use the same tape cassette over and over again. The quality may not be high, but that is not essential. It is better if you take pictures with both your family and friends because we found that many people send off different nonverbal messages when they are at home than when they are in public. However, if you can only test with your family, do; the information will be useful. Without training you will be able to spot whether you are a mixed-message sender.

Most of those testing themselves will discover that

they send off some mixed messages. Almost all of us
have a few negative nonverbals. I know I became aware
of the fact that I slouched all the time. I also found
myself pointing with a pen when talking, a very annoying habit that turned people off. Some actually jumped
back from me when I did it. I tried to correct both
habits. Although I was not sending a total set of negative messages, I did have a few and I was able to correct
them. I believe that all persons should test themselves.

If there are negative message senders in your company or your family you can help them only if you can
spot them. They have certain telltale characteristics.

Mixed-message senders usually have a hesitant, ten-
tative, nervous speech pattern. These developed because
people often ignore them or cut them off. They don't
complete sentences. They jump in and out of conversations erratically. They'll come into a conversation, interrupt people without meaning to, and then they'll stop
when someone looks at them. They frankly act like the
people they are—people who have received the nonverbal message all their lives, "Why don't you shut up,
nobody wants to listen to you."

They tend to overstate and they repeat themselves.
They are not used to others giving credence to what
they say and they think repetition emphasizes. Instead
of saying, "It is a nice picture," they will say, "It is one
of the most beautiful pictures I've ever seen. It's a mas-
terpiece. I really love it. It's in a wonderful frame." Most
of this is unnecessary. They often finish their statments
with a little smile or grin. They do it all the time. They
don't mean anything by it. They grin when they say,
"Good morning, how are you? It's a nice day. Pass me
the salt." But they also grin when they tell you that
they don't like the report you handed in. And that same
little grin at that moment drives you crazy and makes
them an enemy. In context, the wrong grin is aggravat-
ing, annoying, and destructive.

The other look they have that drives people right up a
wall is the "I have a secret" look. They finish every

statement by moving their lips slightly giving the impression that they're in on a joke that no one else knows. It drives the world crazy and gets them into trouble. Finally, we have the constant smiler. Women are more likely to do this than men. There are people who smile no matter what is going on. There is a news broadcaster in Binghamton, New York, who would smile if she announced World War III. She will never make it as a news broadcaster unless she breaks that habit because nobody is going to trust or believe her. Most of the time she just looks silly, but sooner or later that woman is going to be forced to announce that a bus with children went over a bridge and she is going to smile while doing it. That is going to be the end of her career.

Ironically, when these people match their verbal and nonverbal statements, they sometimes match the wrong ones. They will often have overblown unnecessary statements matched with overblown theatrical body motions. To some, they will appear to be putting on airs. Actually, all they are doing is trying very hard to impress you. Of course, for them that's impossible.

If you know one of these people, you can help him. Depending on your relationship, you can either give him a copy of this book or talk to him about it. But I must warn you that many mixed-message senders cannot recognize the mistakes they're making even when they're pointed out to them. So before you worry about your friends, you should worry about yourself.

Even if you are sure that you are not a mismatched message sender and you don't want to go to the expense of hiring, renting, or buying a video tape machine and camera, I suggest, if you are in a public contact business, that you sit before a mirror for an hour a night for one week and carry on a series of make-believe conversations. Ask your boss for a raise, ask him for a favor, try to talk him into doing something, talk to your children, give them an order. If you are a salesman, I would certainly expect you to give your sales presentation to several different types of people. Pretend you are at a party and carry on a conversation with several of your friends. Most people who do this find it very revealing, very enlightening, and sometimes shocking.

Before you attempt it however, we suggest you tell your wife and your family what you are doing because if you don't they may throw a net over you and you may have to practice talking to doctors in a padded cell where there are no mirrors.

6

THE
INTERVIEW GAME
OR
SELLING YOURSELF

I thought long and hard before settling on the title for this chapter. The word "game" bothered me because our research indicates that hard work, effort, and ability—not gamesmanship—are the critical factors in success. However, after I studied what really goes on during interviews, I could not think of any title more appropriate than the "Interview Game." The reason is simple. The people who run interviews make it a game and, what's more, a dirty game.

I interviewed two groups of personnel people while writing this chapter. The first group consisted of sixty-eight men and women from twenty-three different companies. I interviewed ten in their offices, the others at conventions. I found them far more open and honest in cocktail lounges over drinks than they were behind their desks. After a drink or two, they relaxed and openly admitted that they viewed an interview as a game in which an adversary relationship exists between the interviewer and the person being interviewed. The interviewers thought it was their job to catch people lying, to spot them when they were unsure of themselves, and to trap them into admitting personal weaknesses. They looked upon the whole process as a negative one. The only positive aspect of the interview as far as I could see was the ego trip taken by the interviewers. They invariably believed that they could spot a candidate who was lying or lacked self-esteem or who would be inefficient. Unfortunately, the people who get the products of their interviews don't agree with them. I know several large corporations which, after exhaustive studies of their personnel departments, decided they would be better off without them. The only problem is they don't know what to replace them with.

Personnel departments are grossly ineffective because they operate primarily on myth. The criteria they apply to job applicants is unrealistic and stupid and in many cases counterproductive. The only point on which I agree with the people who run personnel departments is that nonverbal messages are often more accurate than verbal ones. Years ago they discovered that job applicants were quite adept at lying and if interviewers listened to what the job applicants were saying they would be fooled much of the time. As a result, the people in today's personnel departments lean too heavily on nonverbal signals and whether an applicant gets a job or a second interview often depends on the nonverbal messages the applicant sends. Interviewers think nonverbal messages are invariably accurate and honest. Of course this is nonsense. One of the strategies I am going to teach you in this chapter is how to lie nonverbally.

I can see some people shuddering at such an immoral suggestion. I agree that nonverbal lying is immoral in most situations. However, not when you are dealing with personnel people who read nonverbal messages inaccurately and make them a basis for judgment. For example, 25 percent of the personnel people we talked to said they would refuse to consider anyone with a wet, clammy handshake for an important position. This is ridiculous, stupid, and unfair. A wet, clammy handshake is often an indication of nervousness and really wanting a job.

Which brings us to the second reason that playing the interview game is not immoral. The people companies hire often are the wrong people. We did a survey of 162 applicants in nineteen different companies. We interviewed them before they went into the interview and when they left. We asked them a series of questions to determine how badly they wanted the job and how much they really wanted to work for that company. We did not rate them on their ability, only their intentions. We found that the people who were most desperate to get a particular job, to work for a particular company, almost never got hired. They were invariably eliminated during interviews. We also discovered that many of the applicants who really didn't give a damn, who already had another job offer, or who were simply out practicing interviewing, scored very well. Obviously, this is not what most companies would want. This amazing fact was verified by a follow-up study in which we questioned people going for job interviews and found that those who already had job offers were far more likely to get a second one. They went into the interviews without the pressure of really needing the job and, as a result, they were more likely to be hired. Many of the nonverbal signs interviewers use to eliminate job applicants were simply signs of nervousness.

We also discovered that many of the nonverbal signs that interviewers believed signaled industry and self-assurance actually identified the applicant as being upper-middle-class. Most interviewers are not aware of this because 90 percent of professional personnel people come from blue-collar backgrounds.

As the system now stands, four types of people have tremendous advantages in job interviews. People who are good-looking have a three to four times greater chance of being hired for almost any position, whether it is typing, sales, or management; it makes no difference at all. If you're beautiful it helps. Second, people from upper-middle-class backgrounds have an advantage. They carry themselves and speak in a manner that tells the interviewers they are self-assured. Third, athletes have smoother, better-coordinated body motions and tend to pass the nonverbal sections of interviews far better than nonathletes. Fourth, actors who are trained at transmitting both verbal and nonverbal messages are absolute experts at getting jobs.

In fact, the actors we encountered were so good at getting jobs that we ran a research project using a half dozen of them, three men and three women. We took resumes originally rejected by client corporations, doctored them, had the actors spend a half hour in the library checking the careers that these resumes were geared to, and sent them out for interviews. They received job offers or offers for second interviews 38 percent of the time—an amazing batting average for people seeking jobs. Their success was based on three facts. First, they dressed the part. Second, they didn't really care if they got the job or not. Third, they knew exactly what the interviewers were looking for and they were able to lie verbally and nonverbally because that's their business. Play and pretend, apparently, is the main criterion for getting hired in America.

I must point out that in most cases in which these people received job offers or second interviews, they were interviewed by people who were professional personnel people. They didn't do nearly as well when they were interviewed by field people working in personnel for a stated period of time. The field people asked an entirely different series of questions and some of them immediately spotted the fact that the actors knew nothing about the field in which they were applying. When the actors were pretending to be engineers, and spoke to another engineer, they were often tripped up almost immediately. I believe this is one of the key weaknesses in personnel departments. The people interviewing often have no concrete concept of the requirements for the job. Since they can't ask factual questions, they set up an artificial criterion and make everyone pass through it on the assumption that if you can beat their criterion you can do anything.

The field men fell into two separate categories. In the first, they simply were brought in from the field to spend twelve to eighteen months in personnel. They usually were given a one-day orientation and then assigned to interview people applying for jobs in their speciality. A second type of field person was brought in and dominated by the vice-president in charge of personnel, put through a mandatory three-week training program, and absolutely forced, unless he had a very strong personality, into obeying the asinine rules which had been set up by the personnel department. In some cases they were even less selective and easier to fool than the personnel professionals. The field men and women left on their own actually applied very sensible criteria to applicants. When we interviewed them, we found they asked themselves several questions about most applicants. First, would this applicant get along with the people he has to work with? If client-contact was part of the job, how well he would relate to the clients was the critical question. If only co-workers were involved, how would he relate to them? Second, is this applicant technically qualified? We found field engineers paid a great deal more attention to the marks the fellow received in engineering than his overall grade average. The people in personnel, on the other hand, paid more attention to the overall grade average than to his marks in engineering. Third, is this person teachable? Almost nobody in personnel asked this question. But it was considered critical by the field people. Does this person look as if he's willing to learn? And the field people, who often had some limited management experience, asked what I considered the most practical question from the company's point of view: is this person worth the money we're paying him? This question was almost never asked by the people in personnel because they had no realistic criteria for judging it. The critical difference here is practical information on how the person is going to be used.

Since the actors did so well in the interviews and since 60 to 65 percent of all people being interviewed are going to have to pass through the personnel screen, we set up a training program for poor interviewees and used these actors as the instructors.

We collected twenty participants identified as poor interviewees—eleven men and nine women. All these people were seeking employment and we explained that if they would cooperate with us we would give them a free lesson on how to get through a job interview. Obviously they had a vested interest in joining the class. I started the session by explaining that we were working on the theory that interviewing was a game and that there were certain verbal and nonverbal rules that could be taught. The men and women doing the teaching were actors and actresses because they were experts at playing nonverbal and verbal games and they were attempting to pass on their expertise to the participants. I then turned the class over to the six actors.

They spent the remainder of the day role playing. First the participants acted out mini-interviews: walking in, sitting down, shaking hands, saying hello, smiling, not smiling, and answering certain stock questions. We took notes. Then the actors and actresses ran through each person's interview as they would have done it. Then we attempted to have the participants copy the actors. By the middle of the day we split the group of twenty into four smaller groups. By three o'clock many of the participants were as good as the actors doing the training. We stopped then because several of the actors had to leave, but we invited anyone who was interested to return the next day to attend a practice session. Only one person couldn't make it and she had a job interview. When we got there the next day we continued the mock interviews, this time under my supervision, with the two actors who returned as coaches. We added one additional training technique. The actors imitated the mistakes made by various participants while that participant played the part of the interviewer. Some of the students found this very helpful.

At the same time, participants met with one of my assistants in another room and she helped them rewrite their resumes. We hired a professional typist to type them and everyone in the class participated in the proofreading session.

These final resumes were also products of research. When we started, we originally intended to use standard guides on resume writing as the basis for our consultation. We found that most of them are written by university professors and personnel directors and are based on limited experience, educated guesswork, or myth. Therefore, we thought it necessary to do some basic research. We enlisted eight companies with twelve personnel officers and their staff. In addition, we enlisted sixty-two executives, who regularly receive resumes, and asked all of those participating to save all the resumes they received from June 1978 to June 1979. We asked each person who read a resume to sign it and make three comments. First, would they bring the person in for an interview? Second, list any mistakes in the resume. Third, list any positive points in the resume.

Surprisingly, the main reasons resumes and cover letters are discarded are spelling, punctuation, and sloppiness. Neatness counts. Often secretaries or clerks go through resumes and screen out those they consider inadequate. This type of screening takes place most often when an executive places an ad for a job in a newspaper and receives 200 replies. Knowing he cannot possibly read that many resumes or interview that many people, he usually has his secretary or some underling go through them to eliminate the unsuitable ones before he sees them. Often the person doing the eliminating has no real idea of what type of employee the company is seeking and will simply throw out those that look amateurish. Obviously, all the advice given by the so-called professionals on typing your own resume is total non-sense. If you are not a good typist, you are a fool if you don't have a professional do it. And even after a professional typist has finished, you should have several friends read it for punctuation and spelling. I also would suggest if there's a word in a resume that has two spellings, take the most common one. Secretaries frequently are unaware of more than one acceptable spelling for a word. We saw several cases of resumes being rejected on that basis alone.

The second most common reason for rejecting resumes is time gaps. Many college professors who write books on how to get jobs indicate that if there is a gap in your work history you cover it with a narrative resume. We found that in most cases narrative resumes don't even get you an interview. When they do, the first question asked is to explain the gap in your resume. If you hesitate, fumble, or fall on your face, you're caught. If you give a quick, glib answer, or lie, you're caught anyway because that's the one thing they check on. Most companies do not check very carefully on resumes and personnel directors are notoriously poor in this regard. But they will check on something you say that isn't on paper.

If you have an extended, unexplainable gap in your resume, you are frankly going to have to fudge. There are several ways you can go about this. You can take the job you had prior to your gap in time and extend it to cover the gap. You can take the job you had after the time gap and push back the starting date. Whatever you do, don't extend both. The fewer cover-ups you allow the better off you are. If you cannot extend the time you spent on a real job, you're going to have to create a fictitious position. The fiction that personnel people run across most often, and the one they're least likely to believe, is that you were self-employed. Unless you have extensive documentation to back this up, it will not work. The best way of covering a time gap is to have a real employer improvise for you. If your uncle, aunt, cousin, father, or anyone else you know, owns a small corporation, even if that corporation exists only on a letterhead, you can claim you worked for them—provided, of course, they're willing to back you up. If you don't know anyone who owns a company and if you spent a year or two at a country club such as San Quentin and you're absolutely sure that telling a potential boss would eliminate you from the job, you're going to have to do some creative writing. The best example I ever saw was a young man who did spend two years in prison. He looked up the name of an Iranian company right after the Ayatollah took over. He then checked and found out that no matter who you wrote to in that company, nobody answered. So he proceeded to create a position and a salary and filled it in on his resume. He even credited himself with completely reorganizing the accounting department, which elminated the third most popular reason for throwing resumes in the circular file. People who write resumes that simply indicate where they were without telling what they did, are hardly ever selected for interviews.

When you're filling out your resume, you don't list simply where you were, you have to list what you did. Putting down "Joe's Shoe Manufacturing Company from 1965–1970, salesman," is a very poor idea. If you put down "Joe's Shoe Manufacturing Company, 1965–1970, salesman" and indicate that you sold more shoes than anyone else in the company, that will catch everyone's attention. Even the fact that you didn't sell too many shoes isn't important because they're not even going to try to check on it. They already know Joe's Company won't give out internal information—what you've told is noncheckable. Then, if you spent from 1970 to 1975 in Sam's Shirt Company as their production chief, you list chief, and say you increased their button supply by 20 percent and cut their costs by 15 percent. Again, this may be complete nonsense, but it dresses up your resume even further. If you claim that when you moved to Harry's Suit Company you personally saw to it that all the suits fitted perfectly, you have window-dressed your resume to the point where people in personnel will be delighted. It's known as a "can-do" and "has-done" resume; created terms for something that is probably fiction.

We know it's fiction because we went through 163 resumes and spotted a series of statements just like those described. Because we have contacts in corporations, we were able to go back and check on forty-three of them. We found that of the forty-three, twenty-four were correct and the others were total fiction. Half of the fiction writers were in good positions and performing on a very high level. In fact, three of them were so high in corporations we decided that we better take that research report and deep-six it. They were high enough up that the truth wouldn't kill them, it would kill us.

The fourth most common reason for not getting an interview is because the resume never even gets read. Resumes that run more than a page, unless they are for executive positions, are often ignored. We found a substantial percentage of personnel people who never read more than a page. They gave us all sorts of excuses for it: if the man couldn't summarize in one page what he did, he wasn't doing it correctly; three- and four-page resumes were unspeakably long and unnecessary and proved the job applicant didn't know what he was doing in the first place. I suspect, after speaking to some of these personnel people, that in their entire lives they never read anything longer than a page.

The fifth reason resumes are rejected is that the resume doesn't indicate you'd fit the job. This doesn't mean that you're not qualified. In many cases, custom tailoring your resume to suit a particular position will overcome this. Having a custom-tailored resume always increases your chances of getting the job provided that you make very sure that the custom-tailored resume is as carefully checked as the mass-produced one for neatness, spelling, and punctuation. As you move up the corporate ladder, custom-tailored resumes are far more productive than mass-produced ones. I do not recommend mass-produced resumes for executive positions.

After you finish your resume, you should write your cover letter. The reason you write the cover letter after the resume is that the cover letter is an advertisement for the resume. In order to write the advertisement, you have to know the product. Good cover letters always have four characteristics. First, they're short. Second, they're simple. Third, they're catchy. And fourth, they're neat. The mistake people most often make in cover letters is simply writing a repeat of the resumes. The letter is supposed to tell a few things about you and get people interested enough to read your resume. The cover letter is an ad for the resume and it can be an ad for you.

I think the best cover letter I ever ran across came from a woman applying for a job as secretary at my company. She sent a letter that was perfectly typed and it said, "You know I don't have a great deal of experience, and I know I've worked for several companies in the last few years and that may not look good. But I guarantee you one thing. If I do come to work for you I'll work like hell!" First I was put off by her choice of language but then I was struck by the honesty, the power, and the forcefulness of the letter. It really had caught my eye. I took a chance and hired her. She did work like hell. She spelled like the devil, showed up when she felt like it, and gave everyone around her a lot of heat. As a result I had to let her go in a few weeks. But she did know how to sell herself in a cover letter.

Assuming you've written a suitable resume and cover letter you will be invited to interview with a number of companies. The minute you receive this invitation, there is a series of steps you should undertake. First, go to a library and do as much research on the company as possible. Find out what their problems are, what their goals are, who their competitors are. Find out as much as you can about their product line. If you can, read the financial statements. Make sure you find out who the president and the vice-presidents of the company are, or at least who's in charge of the area where you're interviewing. Check on whether that person has written anything. If he has, read it or at least skim through it. This will enable you to speak intelligently about the company and its top people during the interview.

The day before the interview, call and confirm the time, place, and the name of the person conducting the interview. With most organizations, calling ahead to confirm will be a plus on your chart even before you arrive. Before you leave for the interview, carefully scrutinize your appearance. Make sure you are dressed suitably, that your breath is clear, your shoes shined, and that you're not wearing too much lipstick or makeup. I know some readers may be insulted by this advice but my survey of interviewers indicates that 9 percent of the young men and women with college degrees eliminate themselves from job consideration by breaking basic grooming rules. I pointed out in my *Dress for Success* series that more than 30 percent are eliminated because of inappropriate clothing.

Make it a point to reach the building or the area of the interview ten to fifteen minutes ahead of time. Make this half an hour if you're interviewing in a major city where traffic can delay you. You can *never* be late for an interview. Being early serves two purposes. It guarantees you're going to get there on time and gives you a last chance to check yourself in the men's or ladies' room before the interview. Even if you were beautifully put together before you left home, it is easy to become disheveled on the way to an interview.

The interview starts the moment you walk into the waiting area. The receptionist in most corporate waiting areas will report to the interviewer on how you approach her and how you impress her. Make it a point to be polite and businesslike. When you've finished telling her you have an interview at one o'clock with Mr. So-and-so, she will probably ask you to take a seat; if not, wait half a minute and then simply do it on your own. If there's a place to hang your coat, hang it. If not, take it off and carry it over your arm. Most interviewers are more impressed by someone who is carrying a coat than someone still wearing one.

Once you have finished announcing yourself to the receptionist, sit down. Pick up one of the company magazines and start reading. Don't take out a book or magazine or anything else you brought with you. It is considered inappropriate. While you're sitting there try not to think about the interview. I know many books on this subject tell you to run over the interview in your mind but that should have been done earlier. Don't fidget. Try not to look overly concerned or nervous. Don't look up from your magazine every three or four seconds or the minute anyone comes into the room. Force yourself to read an article and try to become involved in it. If you must play little mental games with yourself while you're sitting there, tell yourself you're going to get the job. There's nothing the interviewer can do to stop you. He's very lucky that you've arrived. Try to build up your confidence rather than worry about making mistakes.

After you've sat there ten or fifteen minutes (they will often leave you waiting that long to see if you're going to become nervous or jittery), the official interview will usually start in one of two ways. The secretary may call to tell you the interviewer will see you and direct you to his or her office. Most probably, the interviewer will come out to meet you. When the interviewer arrives, stand up and walk toward him. Don't jump up and act nervous. Stand up and set yourself. This means that you pause a tenth of a second to pull yourself together once you get into a standing position. It's a trick that models use. When they get up out of a chair they pause for a split second to compose themselves, and rise to their full height before they walk. Do the same; it will give you a composed look. Walk directly over to the interviewer and shake his or her hand. If you're nervous and your hands tend to sweat, have a little bit of absorbent paper or cloth or something with powder or rosin on it in your pocket or pocketbook. Dry your hand just before you shake the interviewer's hand. If the interviewer comes out to meet you, there are two possible techniques he will use. He will either walk to his office and have you follow him or he will send you to his office. If he sends you to his office and tells you he'll be there in a minute, you must be aware of the fact that he's watching you. Your carriage is extremely important. You're going to be judged by how energetically you carry yourself. We had one gentleman who had a great deal of difficulty walking in a way that made him look energetic. One of the actors finally solved the problem. He had him walk down the hallway as if he were about to receive a gold medal in the Olympics. He imagined himself an athletic, energetic person about to be awarded a medal in front of a large, standing audience. With that in mind he walked more erect, more aggressively, and tested beautifully.

The interviewer is much more likely to send a woman ahead of him. He will often place himself in the doorway at one point so you have to squeeze past him. Many women become upset by this because it seems as if he's getting too close to them too quickly. It almost appears to be a sexual advance. I assure you they'll do the same thing with men. What he's doing is smelling you. He wants to see if you're wearing too much perfume or if you have body odor or bad breath. It is another one of those very unfair interviewing techniques.

When and how an interviewer watches you move is really not important. They're all interested in the same look. When we interviewed them they used such words as "alert," "aggresive," "forceful," and "energetic" to describe the ideal carriage. However, when we showed them pictures, we found the term they were really looking for was "upper-middle-class." They were not able to articulate this because people tend to be myopic when they look up the socioeconomic ladder and have 20–20 vision when they look down. Since nine out of ten personnel people come from blue-collar backgrounds, they do not recognize that the body carriage that is so attractive to them is the product of class.

If you fake a walk for the interview, you may or may not get away with it. Some people have a natural gift for drawing themselves to their full height and looking as if they walk that way all the time. Others make it look very artificial. We found that everyone who practices for two or three hours before a mirror can carry it off for those few moments. If you practice longer, as we suggested in our chapter on socioeconomic level, you will have no difficulty with it at all.

The other possibility is that you will be sent into the interviewer's office and you'll walk in and find him sitting behind his desk. If, when you walk in, he asks you to sit down, do so. If you find yourself standing in front of his desk without his looking up, he's trying to make you feel uncomfortable and test your reaction. The minute you do begin to feel uncomfortable, sit without his permission. Don't feel nervous about it. You've passed another part of the test. When you sit down, you have to remember to keep yourself erect. One of the things we found while training people is that if they had sloppy carriage when they walked, we could train them to walk erectly, but the minute they sat down, they slouched and destroyed their image. You must sit with your shoulders back if you're a woman.

Although you have taken the lead in the nonverbal part of the interview and seated yourself without permission, under no circumstances should you *talk* before he does. Wait for him to start the verbal part of the interview no matter how long it takes. There are some interviewers who will make you sit there an almost interminable period of time waiting for you to blow it. Don't.

By far the silliest piece of folklore and mythology in personnel departments is eye contact. Almost every personnel type I met swore by eye contact. They noticed immediately whether a man or a woman had good firm eye contact and they swore they could tell a great deal

by the way a person handled eye contact. There may be
some degree of truth in it. There have always been
stories of shifty-eyed people. But I've taken this with a
grain of salt for the past forty years. When I was three
and a half or four, my grandmother, a lovely old lady
who wished to lead me into good habits, told me there
was no way I could look her in the eye and tell a lie. It
wasn't a day or two later that I found out it was possible
to do both things simultaneously. As a child I took
great pleasure in proving it. I would take a cookie right
in front of her, eat it, and then deny I had eaten it while
staring her unflinchingly. I loved it, until she hauled
off and gave me a whack where, as she said, it would do
me the most good. After she gave me a little smack in
the rear we laughed because we both understood that at
that early age I had passed a milestone. I understood
you could stare someone in the eye and lie. One of my
childhood myths had been destroyed. Unfortunately for
the people who are being interviewed and the corporations who are getting the product of these interviews,
the people in personnel have not discovered that very
salient fact.

The idea that you can't keep good eye contact while
telling a lie is of course total nonsense. Good liars do it
all the time. Several of the actors, when I told them this
truism, practically fell off their seats laughing. They
made a point during interviews of telling the most atro-
cious lies and staring at the personnel person very
intently while they did it. They found that some of these
men actually believed them.

As a result of this we sent several executives, who
themselves were wonderful interviewers, into personnel.
They, with even greater skill than the actors, lied like
troopers and got away with it. They pretended to be
electrical engineers with doctorates, sociology professors, psychologists, and almost anything under the sun
and no one ever questioned them. Several of them were
hired by their own companies for jobs they were certainly not qualified to do—which caused a bit of a stir in

personnel. Most of the men had offers for second interviews. We found the best tactic during an interview is to look the interviewer directly in the eye. Interviewers insist it proves self-assurance, honesty, integrity. In our opinion, and in everyone else's, it's simply another example of the stupidity of the system.

Now I'm not saying that you can beat every interviewer playing by these rules. There are enough with the good common sense to play their instincts. They don't abide by the silly game I've laid out. But a large enough percentage of them have this fanatical belief in such an abysmally stupid system that it's almost a sin not to take advantage of it.

If you think the nonverbal part of the interview is stupid, the verbal part is ludicrous. During every interview you will be asked a series of indefinite questions. Why do you want to work for this company? Why do you want this particular job? Have you any plans if you get the job? It doesn't make any difference what question they ask. The answer they want is always the same. The answer is the "can-do" answer. They will smile and hire you if you say I want to work at this company because I can do X, Y, and Z. If you give them a realistic set of goals that fit the job, you're likely to get it. I believe I can help this company accomplish its sales goals. I believe I can sell widgets, computers, or anything else. This is what they're looking for, a can-do attitude. If they ask what you liked about your last company, answer that the job there allowed you to accomplish this, accomplish that, accomplish the other thing. If they ask you what you think your life has meant up to now, mention your wife, children, and painting your house, and you're not going to be hired. So you have to pretend that your family isn't the center of your life. They want to hear what you did on your last job and how you really made that company fly. Of course it's probably nonsense. But that's what's going to get you a job. Your answer to every question should be nothing more than a litany of things you have done or things you plan to do. When it's what you plan to do, be specific and realistic within the framework of what you know of the job they're offering. One thing you can't do is smoke, even if you're offered a cigarette. Offering a cigarette is another silly game. If you take it and light up, even after they do, you lose. You also don't criticize past employers. If you worked for the Mafia, you must praise them as equal opportunity employers.

When they ask about hobbies, you must tell them the only hobbies you enjoy are active ones. You're a doer. You don't read books, go to the opera, or watch television. You participate in sports, particularly status sports such as golf or tennis. You're not an observer, you're an active participant. In their opinion, people who read books and go to the opera are losers, while people who play golf and tennis are winners. Of course this is nonsense, but it's the nonsense they're looking for.

If you're still nervous about going to interviews, calm down. Interviewers are really nothing to be afraid of. The reasons you fear interviews are the same reasons egomaniacs behind the desk are having so much fun. They really think it's their game. You wouldn't be afraid of interviewers if you knew as much about them as I do. First, four out of five of the men in personnel graduated at the bottom of their class. They're not as bright as you are and they're not as articulate. They're simply playing in their own ball park. They often are the exact opposite of the people they pretend to be looking for. They're not go-getters. They're never going to be president of their company. Personnel tends to be a dead-end job. They play these little power games, and since it's the only power game they're ever going to play, they take it very seriously. But they are playing a game, and once you understand the rules you can beat them at it. If the information in this chapter does not give you all the confidence you need, we still have a solution. Hypnosis.

We sent several people to doctors who taught them self-hypnosis. They were people who became excessively nervous during interviews. I learned the technique some time ago while trying to improve my concentration. It's a wonderful way to calm yourself and control your emotions. Each and every one of our nervous job candidates, after a series of hypnosis sessions, was able to approach interviews from a new perspective and give a topnotch performance.

7

SALES

When we asked the wives, husbands, friends, and associates of some of the most successful men and women in America to describe them, the word they used most often was supersalesman. In spite of the fact that more than 85 percent of the people being described never held a job in direct sales, they sold all the time. They were more politicians than patriarchs and most of those around them responded to their charismatic personalities rather than their power.

When I told these executives that most of their associates saw them primarily as salesmen, they were in most cases flattered. In fact, two of them suggested an experiment. They sent select middle-management people through my sales training program to see if it would improve their performance. The results were so positive that several of our corporate clients now send all their middle managers to our sales training course.

I believe as do these executives that basic training in sales will enhance anyone's chances of succeeding. That is the reason that this chapter contains more factual data on how to sell than any five books I've read. While I advise that everyone read this chapter, I would suggest that anyone in sales read it a dozen times and anyone in sales training commit it to memory. The research on sales that follows represents a breakthrough.

The one thing that all the best and the worst sales forces have in common is that 20 percent of the people do 50 percent of the work. The reason for this is simple. If you take 100 salesmen with basic product knowledge and train them for five years, twenty will be very competent while the other eighty will be order takers. If you take the same sales force and put them in the field without training, at the end of six months to a year, twenty will be great salesmen and the other eighty will be order takers. Which is a bit surprising, because if you spend five years training men to be engineers, bricklayers, doctors, accountants, or almost anything else, you find that their achievement scores at the end of their training period will generally fall on a bell curve. Although some will perform at a higher level than others, the tremendous discrepancy that is seen in salesmen between those who are successful and those who are unsuccessful will not exist.

There is only one place where you will find similar statistics, and that's in our school system. If you look at good school districts, usually suburban ones, where learning and teaching do take place, you will find test scores

Picture 6

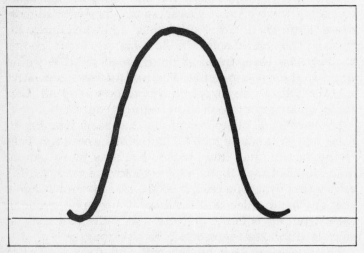

Bell curve. Shows even distribution of
learning in most training situations.

are similar to those in law, medicine, plumbing, and so on. There will be a small percentage of very talented students at the top and a small percentage at the bottom showing little academic talent. But most of the students will be clustered toward the middle. Those in the middle will be a product not of talent, but of training. They will achieve at a level sufficiently high so that most of them will be able to get into a college and just about all of them will perform well in our society. They will become solid middle-class citizens, and their educational abilities, no matter how limited, will be sufficient for them to survive. On the other hand, if you look at the worst schools in our educational system, those in ghetto areas where little or no teaching or learning goes on, you will find that a surprising 20 percent of the students score well on tests, that they progress fairly well through the educational system, and that they succeed at a level comparable to the 80 percent in the suburban schools. If you look at a curve of their accomplishments, it is almost identical to that of salesmen. The reason is simple. Teaching takes place in neither system. In the ghetto, as in sales, students tend to be looked upon as expendable. Those with natural talent survive while the others are thrown to the wolves. Both systems ruin the lives of 80 percent of the people who go through them.

While those teaching at inner-city schools can point to lack of money, background, and motivation of their students as a reason for failure, those teaching salesmen cannot. It is a flaw in the sales training rather than a flaw in the students. There are many reasons why sales training doesn't work. The main one is that professors in our major business schools have always looked down their noses at sales, sales training, and salesmen. They think of salesmen as men in loud suits telling funny jokes, peddling from door to door. Even at the best universities they are not aware of the sophistication of sales. They seem to have the mistaken idea that training in marketing produces an officer corps while sales training produces the infantry. As a result major business schools never encourage their people to go into sales and they have not bothered to research sales training. This puts the people doing sales training in a very unfortunate position. They are forced to guess at what works and what does not. With such a system they have limited success.

Another problem is that the trainers really don't believe in the training. We interviewed sixty-two sales trainers, guaranteed complete confidentiality, and signed nondisclosure agreements with built-in financial rewards if we revealed anything they said. As a result, we received very honest answers. Sixty of the sixty-two said that it was absolutely impossible to train someone who didn't have a natural talent for sales. Of the same sixty, fifty-eight said that even if they didn't train their best students, those with natural ability would catch on sooner or later. In their opinion, the whole point of training is to speed up this catching-on process. It has nothing to do with teaching how to sell, it's simply a way of teaching the students to use their natural abilities more efficiently and more quickly.

Sales training also fails because many sales trainers believe that there is but one correct way to sell. Most sales trainers we talked to have successfully sold insurance, computers, or used cars and they believe in their personal approach. Most of them thought that if a salesman or saleswoman did exactly what they told them to do, they would succeed. When we pointed out to them that the world reacts differently to different people, the majority dismissed that fact as being inconsequential. When we further pointed out that training women to sell the same way a man sells could be counterproductive, sixty-one of the sixty-two said they had heard that before, but in their opinion it was nonsense.

The only one who disagreed, to no one's surprise, was a woman. She said she was teaching women to sell the way she sold, and that they were far more effective than those trained by men. She believes that traditional sales training works only for men. Our statistics on women in sales back her up completely. The sales training women get in most corporations is counterproductive. If you take 100 women and train them to sell insurance, computers, or anything else, using the standard methods that most of the major corporations who spend millions on sales training use, only eight to twelve of those women will be productive salespeople. The rest will be order takers. If you take the same women and put them in the field without training, as is often done in real estate and insurance, they will outperform the males by 20 percent. Obviously, the sales training women get destroys their natural ability to sell. The present methods of sales training do not work with women because they are based on the assumption that women sell the same way men do, which of course is nonsense. The one characteristic we found to be common to all the great saleswomen was that they are all very independent women who take their training with a grain of salt.

Every one of them said that their male sales trainers told them to keep good eye contact or they would turn their buyers off, but the women knew that keeping good eye contact would turn their buyers on. Several of them pointed out that their instruction in nonverbal communication had them handling a contract in a way that was very sexy. But the silliest advice any of them received was to smile all the time. Two women, one who sold computers and one who was an attorney, said that if they smiled nobody took them seriously. One predicted the results of our research before we started. She said, "Smiles kill sales." If a woman smiles they ask her, "What's a nice girl like you doing in a job like this?" And since being taken seriously is the main problem women have in business, they must start by looking serious. Never smile for at least the first ten minutes of the first meeting until you've established the fact that you're a serious business person.

The universal advice from successful saleswomen is that women should pay no attention to their male sales trainers. They should obey their instincts when it comes to eye contact and body language. In addition, they think women have several advantages. A woman can be far more aggressive than a man when dealing with a male. In fact several of them suggest that their success was partially the result of the inability of most men to say no to a persistent woman. They also believe that most women learned basic techniques when they were young, while boys did not. The only warning they give to women is always be feminine. Don't try the macho close, which is, "I'm in charge here and you'll do what you're told."

Their recommendation is that companies design a new sales course for women. My recommendation is that companies redesign all their sales training. Our research found that sales depends as much on nonverbal communication as verbal and although some companies think they give nonverbal sales instruction, they really don't. The simplest proof is that they give the same training to women as they do to men. The instruction they give is based on untested assumptions and is often contradictory. In some sales training programs, individual instructors bring their own personality to bear. If you get one set of instructors you are taught to sit up straight while another swears you must lean forward to sell. Both are wrong. The truth is you must present a single socioeconomic sales message.

I do not contend that all sales training is a total waste of time. I am convinced that some of the better sales training programs do positively affect sales. But they do so without teaching anyone to sell. The success element has more to do with management than sales. The sales instructors are correct, they can teach a good salesperson to sell more quickly. I am not suggesting that major corporations close their sales training departments, but I do think they should upgrade and expand them. Some of their techniques are very productive.

The most successful technique in sales training is the motivational meeting. Outsiders may laugh at full-grown men and women running around in funny hats cheering for their company or department the way they did for their high school teams. They laugh because they do not understand.

It has nothing to do with teaching them to sell. Its object is to get people in the right state of mind so that they will sell. A man who sells 100 widgets a week may sell 110 if you can get him all excited about selling widgets. A second man who normally sells ten widgets may sell eleven if you get him excited. Motivation never makes a ten-widget salesman a 100-widget salesman and no one claims it does, but motivational programs have bottom-line value.

When we looked at the production of sales forces after a good motivational program, we found increases. The results could be traced in an S-curve with the first part of the S bigger than the second part. A 100-widget salesman, for example, might increase his sales by ten widgets a week for six weeks. At the end of this six-week period his sales would slump for about three weeks. But the down side of the curve was smaller than the up side, and, as a result, although he lost eighteen sales the last three weeks, he gained sixty for the first six weeks and therefore increased his sales by forty-two. With that type of increase, it is worthwhile for most companies to conduct motivational meetings on a regular basis. The end product—a motivated salesman and a motivated sales force—makes sense because motivated sales forces have a higher base line than unmotivated ones.

The next productive area of sales training is product knowledge. All the statistics indicate that once a man has basic product knowledge, additional technical expertise is not necessarily productive. Surprisingly, this is as true when selling computers as when selling insurance. Now I'm not implying that anyone can sell computers or insurance unless he understands the product. However, men and women are most likely to buy from salespeople who are on the same intellectual and technical level that they are. Knowing a bit more than your client does is good. Knowing too much more than your client does will kill a sale. Brilliant technical salesmen usually confuse the buyer, not sell him.

The third area of sales training that tested as being productive is time management. Salesmen, including some very good ones, are notoriously disorganized. When dealing with the entire sales force, this is the area that tends to have the greatest long-range positive impact. The area which will have the greatest impact with individuals, however, is client analysis. Teaching salesmen

Picture 7

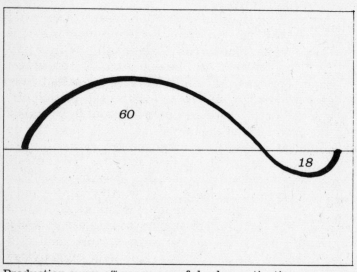

Production curve after a successful sales motivation program.

to use varied approaches depending on whom they're dealing with is very helpful, particularly if the salesman handles a high-ticket item and sells to corporations. It can turn a third-rate order taker into a major producer in industries in which corporate approach is critical. However, we found only the very best sales trainers and training programs cover this subject adequately.

And finally, the heart and guts of present sales training courses is the prepackaged verbal presentation. Most major companies teach their salesmen a standard presentation. These standard presentations vary greatly; some are effective and some very ineffective. The most effective ones use sound teaching principles. They give an audiovisual presentation whenever possible, they keep it simple, and they steer their technical salesmen away from jargon. They organize the sale into a series of digestible intellectual bites. They think for the salesperson. They protect him from himself. They attempt to answer all the questions with the standard presentation. In addition, they have prepackaged answers to often-asked questions. One of their best sales techniques is called "straw man." The salesman leaves a hole in his presentation knowing the buyer will question that part. Naturally, he has the perfect answer.

There are two sound psychological principles that most great salespeople use. The first is the "Yes Principle." If you ask people to commit to anything, their first reaction is to say no. Therefore, you have to get them into the habit of saying yes first. Most readers will recognize the insurance version of the yes principle, because insurance salespeople are best known for using it. They will often ask a client such questions as: "You do want your wife and children to have the same life-style that they have now if anything happened to you?" Obvious answer: yes. "You would want your children to be able to go to the same fine schools they're going to now?" Obvious answer: yes. "I'm sure that you would want your wife and children to be able to live in this house if anything happened to you?" And this obvious yes answer leads to the critical question which is often a statement. "Therefore, you must want this policy that guarantees all that." To which a client is more likely to answer yes because he has given three yes answers in a row. This approach recognizes the fact that thinking and answering are matters of habit and if you can get people into a routine or path of positive or negative answers, they are likely to continue on the same path.

The second effective strategy is joining the opposition. Great salespeople almost never argue. No matter what the person they're selling to says, they begin by agreeing with it. If the buyer says that the house they're selling is the most expensive house they've seen in that neighborhood, they say, "Yes, it is very expensive and I can understand your not wanting to pay that much. However. . . ." Or if the buyer says that the house they're selling has beige carpets and they can't stand the color beige, the good salesperson will say that he or she dislikes beige, too, and understands how the buyer feels. However, beige would go with the furniture the buyer has now, and it's a universal color. The classic example of this technique was used time and time again by good salesmen when they answered the price question, "Why does yours cost more than the other fellow's?" A good salesman always starts by saying, "I understand your asking that question. It's a normal question. You should be concerned about price. The reason ours cost more is our product has A, B, C, and D and theirs does not." Poor salesmen invariably say, "The reason ours is more expensive is A, B, C, and D," without first agreeing that the question had legitimacy. One of the first rules of sales is never disagree with the buyer. Always start by agreeing with him and then show him why he's wrong.

Once a good salesperson has eliminated a prospect's objections, the intent is to get him to sign on the dotted line. Salespeople, at least the good ones, are always looking for commitment. If they are not sure that a prospect is ready to commit, they use a technique called the trail close. They ask the prospect if he wants his new product shipped by rail or by air, or whether he wants it in blue or green. No matter what answer he gives, if it indicates that he wants to buy, they hand him a contract. If the prospect objects, they continue to sell, always with the same object in mind: commitment. Good salesmen always ask for the sale and poor salesmen don't.

The techniques I have just described can help you sell

anything, including yourself. They can help you get a raise, a promotion, a new job, and they can help you get others to do what you want them to do, but they will help you only if you are in the lucky 20 percent. Our research finds that these techniques work only for 20 percent of most sales forces although 45 percent or more try to use them. The people for whom they work are no better-looking, no more aggressive, no more earnest, no more trustworthy than the people who don't sell.

Our research shows that these techniques work only when they are combined with the proper nonverbal selling system. The nonverbal element in sales is the real key to success. This discovery came about as the result of a major research project in which we video taped salespeople making actual and simulated sales presentations. My staff studied more than 1,800 hours of tapes in an attempt to identify the characteristics of each group. The study was conducted with the cooperation of thirty-four companies. Some of the companies put cameras in their own offices and photographed people trying to sell to them. Others set up elaborate simulated sales sessions and had them video taped by professionals in studios while others sent us homemade video tapes.

Our original plan was to have only the people on my staff look at the video tapes. We soon discovered that people in specific industries saw things in presentations that people outside the industry did not. We therefore revised our research method for the first time. Instead of having the tape sent to us, we first had them viewed by people in the same industry, usually the executives in charge of the sales force, and had them comment on the verbal and nonverbal characteristics of their good and poor salespeople. Sixty percent of the information we have in this chapter is based on their comments.

When the tapes were sent to us, our researchers looked at them and reported on the differences they noticed between the good salespeople and the poor ones. We followed a standard procedure. First, the tapes were played without sound. This helped our researchers isolate the nonverbal elements of the presentation. Then they listened to the verbal presentation without the picture. Finally, they looked at the video tape with picture and sound and made an independent set of comments each time.

We found that this research procedure had several built-in flaws. The main one was that it broke the researchers into visual and verbal camps. They tended to defend their positions. Our solution was to take the original seven-person research team and divide it. We added two additional researchers, which gave us three three-person teams. Each team specialized. If the team saw the visual part of tape four, they would get to hear only the verbal part of tape five and the combined assignment on tape six. We didn't want them defending any one point of view. We wanted independent analysis of each part that was not prejudiced by what they had previously seen or heard. This produced more realistic results.

The first thing that struck everyone who looked at the tapes was that the good salespeople were calmer. Their body movements were smooth and unhurried. They made no jerky motions, particularly when they were handing a contract or a pen across the table. They didn't surprise anyone, they did everything gradually, they never pulled a rabbit out of a hat. When they went into their briefcases to get a paper, they knew exactly which paper they were picking up, yet they flipped through one or two before slowly picking out the one they needed.

We also identified people who never sold. We called them the jumpies. The jumpies were people who seemed to be very nervous. They moved their hands and mouths too quickly. They gave the impression that they were upset and they communicated this to the buyer.

There is a phenomenon called mirroring. If one person in a room shows signs of nervousness, there is a very definite possibility that the other people in the room will pick it up, particularly if the nervous person is talking. Therefore, if a salesperson is nervous, jumpy, and on edge, the buyer will be put on edge and obviously that's not good.

After three years, we decided we were raising almost as many questions as we were solving. For example, when we first started looking at the tapes, they contained apparently conflicting information. We saw that one group of very successful salespeople tended to, if not touch their clients, come very close to them when they were closing a sale. When we questioned these salespeople, they all made similar comments. They couldn't sell anyone they couldn't touch or get close to. At the same time we noticed that one of the things that killed sales was poor salespeople moving into someone's territory. Although we knew that good salespeople closed in, we didn't know when or how.

As a result, we were forced to do a study on body space and its impact on sales. We gave actual purchasing agents and people who were playing buyers in simulated sales situations one of two devices. One was a hand-held device with a button. The harder you pressed the button, the higher the needle registered. The other was a brake pedal with the same type of apparatus. We told them when they were annoyed to squeeze or press the device and the more annoyed they became the harder they were to squeeze or press.

We then had salespeople approach them and studied their reactions. We found that when a good salesperson appeared they were much less likely to squeeze the button or press the brake. There were a variety of reasons but the main one was that good salespeople have a sixth sense. Without ever knowing the brake was being pressed or the button was being squeezed, they sensed when they were offending people and backed off. Good salespeople didn't come physically close to their clients until they could do it without offending. Sales for them was a process of getting closer, of breaking down barriers. Poor salespeople, on the other hand, invaded other people's territory, touched them in ways that they found objectionable, and turned them off completely.

The sixth sense we talk about is one that can be developed through training. We use several methods. The one that's simplest to describe is one in which we have a salesperson approach an instructor who signals him when he is giving off positive verbal and nonverbal messages. After fewer than a dozen exposures, most salespeople begin to get a feeling for what they can and cannot do.

If you're a salesperson, or someone who has to sell his ideas for a living, you must practice creating a good first impression. Our testing indicates that less than 20 percent of the male and 30 percent of the female population create a positive first impression. We have all met people who immediately make everyone feel good. The object is to become one of those people. The best method for practicing is to get a full-length mirror and try very hard to look upon that person in the mirror as your student. The first twenty-five times you see yourself in the mirror, or the first two or three days, you're not going to like what you see. However, you will begin to get used to that person in the mirror and once you do, you will be able to correct that person's negative message sending. You will discover that you would rather that person hold his or her head at a slightly different angle. You will discover that that person smiles a little too much or not quite enough. You will discover that that person leans forward when shaking hands, which annoys you. You will discover that that person stands at a funny angle or that person's clothing doesn't seem to hang well and simply by observing them you will begin to correct those faults.

In addition to practice with a mirror, you're going to have practice with people. The ideal group is a dozen people, six men and six women, because this will give you more reactors. A reactor is someone who plays opposite the salesperson and reacts to him. During the sale they are to interrupt with constructive criticism. When you shake hands they might say, "Why don't you make it a bit firmer?" Or, "Your grip is a bit too strong for a woman." They are to interrupt you continually, have you repeat an action until you satisfy them. Their job is not to criticize you, it is to coach you. They're to look upon their job in the same way that a golf pro would look upon his. They are to tell you to raise your hand a bit or lower your eyes a bit. If you practice with enough people you are going to get conflicting information. This is because there are several variations of nonverbal messages that you can send out and that one variation will work with one type of person while a second variation works with another. In the same way you now adjust your verbal presentation to suit your client, after training you should be able to adjust your nonverbal presentation.

When two people sit or stand facing each other, the distance between them affects their comfort and their credibility. If two men who are the same size, the comfortable distance for one will be most comfortable for the other; at that point, both will have their highest credibility rating. If the same man meets a woman, he should stand or sit four to six inches closer. Women, when they talk among themselves, stand and sit closer and a man who sits or stands back seems distant. He is less intimate and, as a result, less credible. The reverse is true when a woman is selling to a man. She should sit four to five inches farther back than she would if she were selling to a woman. Her comfort distance is an intrusion upon his territory. If a man is standing and selling to a man who is noticeably shorter than he, he should back off three to four inches. Most of the time this will relax the shorter man. When he's dealing with a woman, the opposite is true. If a man or woman is shorter than the person he or she is selling to, whether the buyer be male or female, the seller should stand as close as possible without arching the neck at an artificial angle, which would cut into his or her credibility.

Picture 8

A. Ideal sales distance when one man sells to another.
Slightly more than an arm's length.

B. Ideal sales distance when one woman sells to another.
Definitely shorter than an arm's length.

C. A man must move in when selling to a woman.

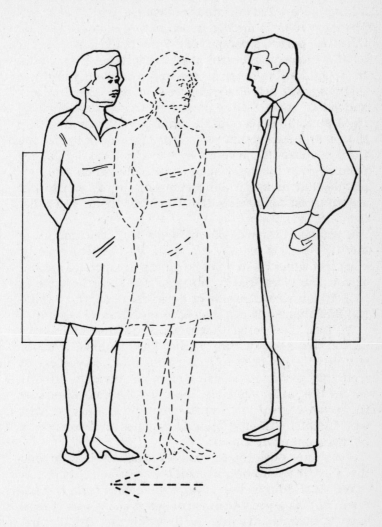

D. A woman must move back when selling to a man.

There are no exact measurements. The distance at which people feel comfortable varies dramatically. The size or the sex of the person and where the meeting is taking place will determine the distance that works best. The most reliable method of estimating distance is from the other person's perspective. You should not guess at what distance you feel the most comfortable. You should try to look at the other person and see where you think their barriers are. Place yourself outside their barriers and make them feel comfortable. If you do, you'll be right 80 to 90 percent of the time. If you're in an office, the general rule is that two thirds of the desk is his, one third is yours. If, however, he has major barriers at the front edge of his desk, such as pen and pencil sets or a plaque that makes it almost impossible for you to put anything on his desk without moving them, you must first ask permission.

If you sit at the side of a person's desk, the amount of territory that is usually his is shown in Picture 12. If you meet someone in a public dining area where neither of you has territorial rights, you can split the table in half. If you sit at the side of a neutral table, the territorial line almost divides the space equally.

We also discovered that physical setting changes a person's concept of body space. For example, a buyer sitting with his back to a corner cannot be approached from his protected sides. You must advance directly across the table. His body space will be determined by the psychological fortress in which he has placed himself. His physical environment becomes an extension of his personal environment.

Sometimes our created sense of space extends beyond the body. If a man or a woman comes from a large city, never touch him or her. If a person comes from a small town, he has a greater sense of space but is less threatened by people invading it. It is for this reason that most people in small towns look upon people from Chicago, New York, and other large cities as being cold and distant when actually they are trying to repect the other

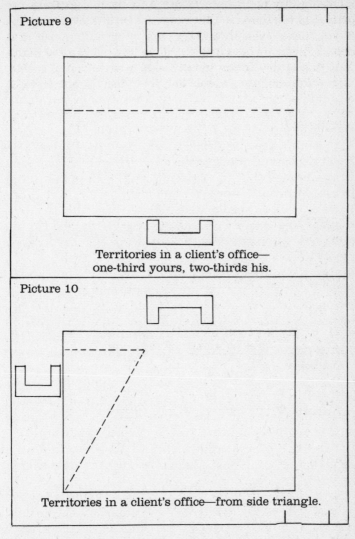

Picture 9

Territories in a client's office—
one-third yours, two-thirds his.

Picture 10

Territories in a client's office—from side triangle.

person's privacy. Ironically, they are being their friend-
liest when they seem least friendly. On the other hand,
people from small towns who come into big cities are
often thought to be rude and pushy when, in actual
fact, they are attempting to be friendly. Touching for

most big-city people starts three to six inches from the body. That is the area they consider intimate body space. If you have lived in a large city, you will notice that people, even in crowded subways and elevators, maintain this three- to six-inch distance whenever possible. When it becomes impossible, they feel uncomfortable

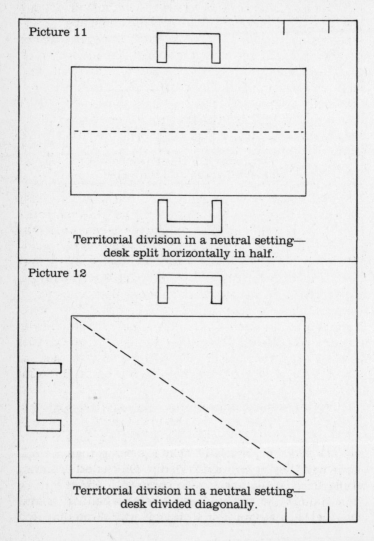

Picture 11

Territorial division in a neutral setting—
desk split horizontally in half.

Picture 12

Territorial division in a neutral setting—
desk divided diagonally.

and become very quiet. If you, without a legitimate reason, come within three to six inches of a person in a big city, you will instantly turn him off. In order to survive in big cities, people have to defend their individuality and this is one of the ways they do it. The only time you get a similar reaction from people in a small town is if you come close to their eyes or their sexual organs. They then feel threatened and become defensive.

The primary rule for a salesperson is never threaten anyone to whom you're trying to sell. This is why most great salesmen, particularly those who are tall, lean back when they stand. Great salesmen are hardly ever physically aggressive, enabling them to be very aggressive verbally. It also explains why lower-socioeconomic body signals tend to be negative in sales. A lower-socioeconomic stance is an aggressive stance, which physically threatens people and kills sales.

Another sure turn-off for most people is being ignored. All great salespeople are great listeners, or at least they seem to be. They give the impression that they are interested only in the customer. When the buyer talks, the salesperson gives rapt attention. You can learn to look interested if you practice in a mirror. However, the body signals are standard. For a man the angle of rapt attention is with shoulders and head arched slightly forward. For a woman, the body angle is greater than for a man. If she sits at the same angle that a man sits at she will appear disinterested. We expect women to lean farther forward when they are listening. Naturally, the normal position for a woman when she's selling is different from that of a man.

There are several mistakes that women make when sitting down. One, they will sit too close to the edge of the chair and two, they will sit with their legs bent to one side. The only effective sitting position for a woman is one with her legs crossed. This requires that a woman wear a skirt at least two inches below her knees.

As in most research projects, one piece of information often led to another. For example, we found that left-

Picture 13

A. Male at rapt attention.
   Can sit up or even lean back.

B. Female at rapt attention.
   Must lean forward.

handed people are more likely to be good salesmen than those who are right-handed. We immediately pulled the tapes and started playing left-handed versus right-handed to see if there were any obvious differences; there were. Left-handed salespeople, if given a choice, would sit or stand to the buyer's left, while right-handed salespeople would sit or stand to the buyer's right. When we asked them why, they said they felt more comfortable there. However, when we tested the buyers, we found right-handed buyers, who make up the majority, usually prefer people on their left. Therefore, if you deal with a right-handed buyer, you should sit or stand on his left, and if you deal with a left-handed buyer, you should sit or stand on his right. Salespeople pick the side on which they feel most comfortable rather than picking the side that makes the buyer feel most comfortable, thereby breaking one of the basic principles of sales. Good salespeople make their buyers feel good.

We noticed that left-handed people also handle pens and contracts differently. While righties often pushed contracts straight across the table, lefties almost invariably handed the contracts at an angle that tested as being less offensive. You can get into a person's body space if you come in sideways moving away from that person. We found the way left-handed people held pens also gave them an advantage. They tended to point the pen at themselves when explaining something on a written contract. Right-handed people often aimed the pen at the buyer making the buyer feel very uncomfortable. People do not like having things pointed at them.

We also discovered that you could tell whether your sale is going well by starting to move in on the buyer. This is the nonverbal counterpart of the trial close we discussed earlier. One of the keys of completing a sale is to physically move in on the other person. If you start to move in and you are rejected, there is a good chance the sale is not working and you should postpone asking for a commitment. Good salespeople, if they are rejected, change direction nonverbally. We noticed that when this occurred they also changed the nature of their verbal

Picture 14

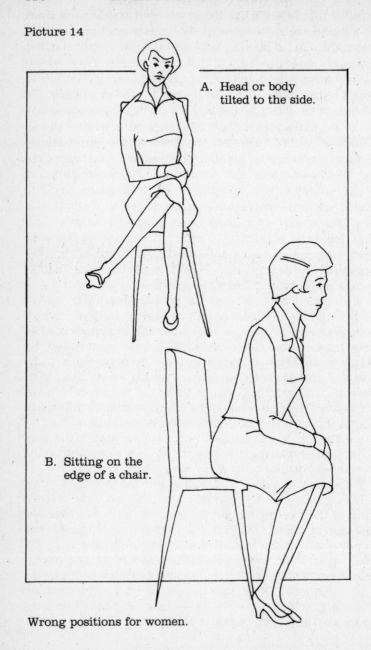

A. Head or body
   tilted to the side.

B. Sitting on the
   edge of a chair.

Wrong positions for women.

Picture 15

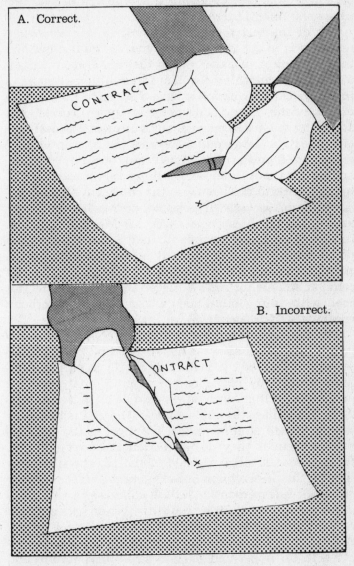

Right and wrong way to handle a pen and a contract.

presentation. They read nonverbal rejection correctly as a signal that they were doing something wrong. They backed off and began moving slowly in again, only this time on a different track.

One of the best methods for moving into someone's territory is to get him to invite you. If you can get him to hold a piece of paper, write his name, read a paragraph, or do anything else that forces him to partake in the physical activity of a sale, you have overcome a major hurdle. If you can't get the buyer involved, you are going to have to move in on your own. The best way is to sneak in. Don't pull a contract out of your attaché and throw it on the desk. Take it out, put it in your lap, and hold it there a minute. Let him see it in your lap, let him get used to it. Then move the contract very nonchalantly onto the table. If possible, do it when he is not looking. Good salespeople never surprise their clients. In fact, if they can arrange it, they will start the sales presentation with a contract lying on the table so the client becomes used to looking at it. One of the key commandments for sales is never surprise anyone, not even with your clothes. Use a very normal, everyday vocabulary; it creates trust.

Which brings us to a very important point: good salespeople have a matched visual, verbal, and product presentation. One of the main flaws with sales presentations created by major corporations is that they are invariably written with upper-middle-class verbal patterns. Sometimes they do not match the products they're selling, which is unfortunate, but most of the time the real problem is they do not match the socioeconomic verbal and nonverbal signals of the salespeople. Very simply, the presentation doesn't sound as if it's coming out of the salesperson's mouth. It sounds as if he's reading something and, as a result, the buyer gets a mixed verbal-visual message which is the surest way to kill credibility. If you are selling an upper-middle-class product with an upper-middle-class sales presentation and you have lower-middle-class verbal-visual patterns, you should take one or two steps immediately. Change your presentation so it matches your normal verbal and visual patterns or change your patterns so they match the presentation. It is preferable to change the presentation because changing your verbal and visual patterns will take many, many months. The other you can do almost overnight.

What you must do is take your presentation and read it onto a tape recorder and then say every sentence over in your own words. Say it as you would say it when speaking to your neighbor. Avoid vocabulary that isn't a normal part of your everyday speech. Do not say "the automobile will positively impact your image," if normally you would say, "the car will make you look great." Only after you've taken this step should you work on upgrading your socioeconomic message system. We don't want you to starve to death while you are doing it.

Good salesmen and good saleswomen do a sales dance. They move to the other person's vibes. They go into the sales situation with the idea of controlling the sales dance. They lead. The whole object is to get the other person to follow. They use all sorts of devices to get the buyer to move the way they want him to move. They first get him to move physically. They never try to sell a product by verbal means only. They're always trying to sell themselves, then their product. Good salespeople recognize that they have to move the buyer's body to move the buyer's mind, which brings us to two major breakthroughs in research.

First, all the research on body signals until mine was based on the premise, stated or unstated, that the mind controlled the body. If a person folded her arms, she was turning you off. As we indicated in an earlier chapter, it's not necessarily true. Our research indicates that in most sales situations it's easier to change someone's body position than to change their mind. And this is the preferred technique used by most good salespeople. They found through trial and error that if you once get a person to change their body position, the mind will follow.

When successful salespeople run across someone who is being offensive or whose physical bearing sends off a very strong negative message, they immediately get off the subject of the sale. They change their verbal tack. They relax their bodies in hopes that the mirror image effect will take place and the buyer will relax his. If this does not work, good salespeople will attempt to change the buyer's position. They will ask the buyer to hold or pick up an object, to help them with a sales prop, to get something from his desk, to get them a piece of paper, or to lend them a pen. Anything to change his physical position. They may also try to change his physical attitude by changing his mental attitude. This is the theory behind the traditional salesman's adage, if you can get a man to laugh, he isn't going to be sitting there staring at you as if he hates you. The object is to put the buyer in a friendly, positive position. When we questioned the better salespeople, some consciously realized what they were doing and others did not. One of the best examples of involving people in a sale came from a real estate saleswoman. She had every paper in her office rolled up in rubber bands like old maps. She said that it was much easier to sell a piece of property after she had the diagram for two days because by that time it would have been rolled long enough so that in order for her to spread it out, the potential buyer had to help hold down the edges. Once she involved the buyer in this way, she was halfway to the sale.

This is a very important lesson for nonprofessional sales people. We photographed at least fifty corporate meetings where people were selling on a one-to-one basis. The unsuccessful businessmen and women usually stood back from the person they were selling and talked at him, a very weak method. The effective business people sold the same way crack salespeople did; they involved the person to whom they were selling in physical activity. They got their prospect, who was often their boss, personally involved in holding charts, pointing to slides, moving his chair, or even passing out papers. By getting him involved, they enlisted his physical aid and they put him psychologically on their side. These people were successful three or four times more often than the people who talked at other people. If you ask your boss to give you a raise, okay a new project, or change your desk, you are selling and you should involve him.

Where you sell can be as important as how you sell. The ideal sales environment is not an office, but a conference room. The table is oval because the curved edges blur territorial lines and make it easier for the salesperson to pass a contract or other printed material to a prospective buyer. In an ideal sales environment the client will be relaxed. He will not get the feeling he's in your office but in his own. One of the ways of accomplishing this is getting him to sit facing the door while you sit with your back to it. This will give him a feeling of safety and command. The best colors for sales conference rooms are beige and blue. They have a relaxing effect.

If you have to sell in your office there are a few essentials. First, if the office is small and it can accommodate only your desk, your chair, and two chairs for guests, the guest chairs must be the right type. There are two types of sales chairs: one with wheels and one with wheels and a swivel and they both move. If you seat a person in a chair that does not move and you come on too strong, he can become extremely defensive which will kill the sale. If you seat him in a chair that does move, he can simply move away from you for a second (a signal you can look for) and that will relax him. Swivel chairs make sales (Picture 17A). Even in a small office there are two possible arrangements: the authority design (Picture 17A) and the nonauthority design (Picture 17B).

A more efficient sales office is the slightly larger one in Picture 17C. In Picture 17C, as in A and B, you always put the prospect in the movable chair. In Office C, the officeholder has two options: to sit behind his desk, be an authority figure, and sell from that perspec-

Picture 16

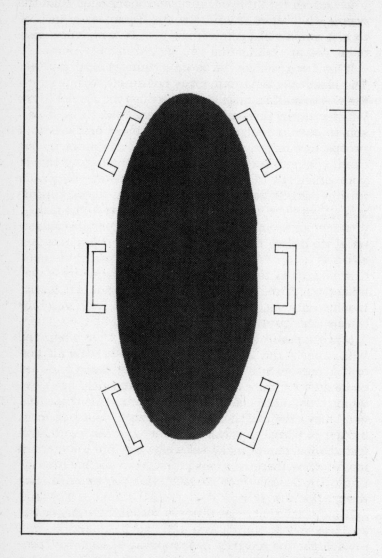

Ideal sales environment. Beige walls, well lit, swivel
chairs with wheels, oval desk.

tive, or to sit on the couch and give the prominent position to the buyer (Picture 17C).

In Picture 18, the two chairs next to the couch and the chairs in front of your desk should be on wheels or swivel and, here again, you may choose where you wish to sit (Picture 17C).

If you are entering the client's office, walk in without hesitating. Never speak until you reach the person's desk. Always introduce yourself with a firm handshake. When you're signaled to sit, sit down, but pause a second beforehand so you don't look rushed or harried. If you have your choice of seats, choose the seat on the left unless you know the person is left-handed, in which case choose the one on the right. If there are barriers in front of his desk that make it impossible for you to place items there, ask to move your seat around to the side. If you have to sell directly across a man's desk, remember the third of the desk closest to you is your territory but ask permission before moving on the remainder of the desk. And finally, don't come in and try to take over immediately. Take command of the situation gradually. If you come on too strong in the beginning, you will offend most buyers.

If you are going to sell to a person in her home, the first thing you do is ask her if you can use the kitchen or the dining room. Most serious family discussions are carried on in those places, not in the living room. The living room is a place for formal entertainment and she will be on her guard there and sit at a distance. In most living rooms the couches and the chairs are four to five feet apart. Your chance of selling anything to a person in her home triples if you can get her into the kitchen. Once you do, however, do not choose a seat. Let her assign you a seat because in most homes the husband and wife have their own seats and will be offended if you take them.

No matter where they sell, good salespeople are professionals; they act like professionals and they think like professionals. They look upon sales as an honored

Picture 17

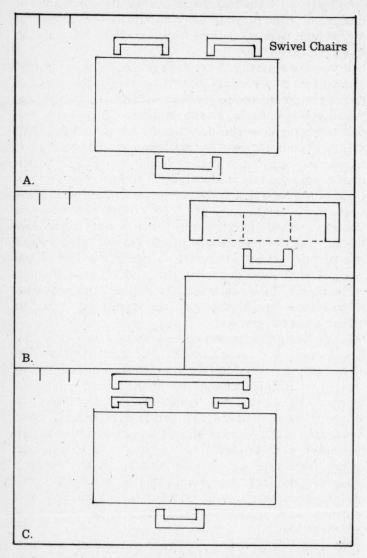

Three variations of small office. A. High authority office.
B. Best sales office. C. Multiple function office.

Picture 18

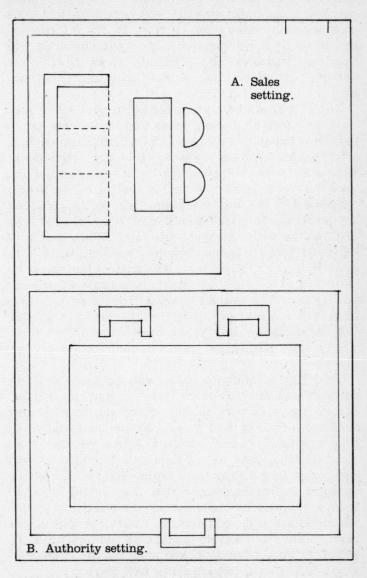

A. Sales setting.

B. Authority setting.

Ideal office design.

profession, which it is. They legitimately try to help their clients whenever they can and they are constantly involved in self-improvement. Good salespeople take sales courses, read books such as this, try the information out to see if it works, and judge for themselves. The poor ones will invariably reject new ideas. They do not believe anything will help because up until now nothing has.

One of the reasons some salespeople can't sell is they have an image of themselves as hucksters. They try to deny this image by taking a dignified, dull approach. It never works. Enthusiasm is one of the characteristics of good salespeople; being excited about one's product and showing real interest is critical to making a sale. Nearly 75 percent of the best salespeople told us they couldn't sell a product they didn't believe in. We wondered why until we started looking at video tapes. When they lied, we could spot it. The salespeople from one large company who didn't believe that their product line was competitive, projected all the classic lie signals when comparing their line to their competition's. They put their fingers up against their noses, they covered their mouths, they looked down, they avoided eye contact. They practically wore signs that said, "I don't believe in my product."

Ironically, confidence men, who you would think couldn't possibly believe in their product, do. I questioned five who were in prison for working various confidence rackets, and four of the five said that when they were talking about a stock or a property, they were convinced they were telling the truth. Two of them said they often forgot they were lying. They would get so wrapped up in their story that they would begin to believe it. One said the only way he could con people was to believe in the con himself. What he described was close to the Stanislavski method of acting—when he was working a mark he looked upon the con as the real world and believed in the part he was playing.

Unlike the people who worked for the company mentioned earlier, confidence men, when their veracity is attacked, react as if they're telling the truth. Unlike the four salesmen from that company, they defend their claims.

In addition, when a buyer attacked one of their claims, they didn't defend them. Good salespeople have a common way of handling an attack. When they believe in their product they let the attacker know in nonverbal ways that they don't agree with him. They erect nonverbal defenses. They hardly ever contradict someone, at least not in the middle of an attack. Instead, they deny the validity of the attack through a series of body signals. When they're sitting at a table, good salesmen steeple and good saleswomen low-steeple.

When sitting in a chair without a desk, good salesmen cross their legs and fold their hands or fold their arms. Good saleswomen will steeple in their laps or fold their arms. These are very critical moves because if someone is attacking your product or your beliefs, and you remain sitting in an open position, you announce nonverbally that you agree with them. No matter what you say, they will never take you seriously.

Poor salespeople and salespeople who are lying often give off the same nonverbal signals for different reasons. People who don't believe in their product and people who don't believe in themselves oversell because they try too hard. They overstate nonverbally. Instead of gestures and expressions being used as positive sales tools, they become negative ones. Poor salespeople offend by gesturing past their normal territorial lines. This is the surest way of killing sales and half the poor salespeople in America do it. See Pictures 20 and 21.

The information in this chapter is quite extensive but it represents only the tip of the sales-research iceberg. Although it will help individual salespeople and some sales trainers, it will not really qualify anyone to teach nonverbal sales. It takes us three to six months to train an experienced sales trainer to teach nonverbal techniques. Anyone who attempts to do it without this train-

Picture 19

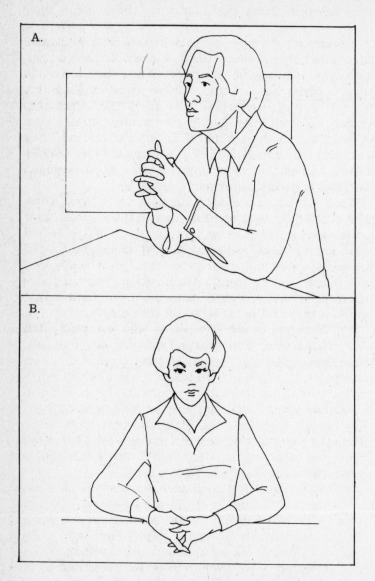

A. Man high steepling. B. Woman low steepling.

Picture 20

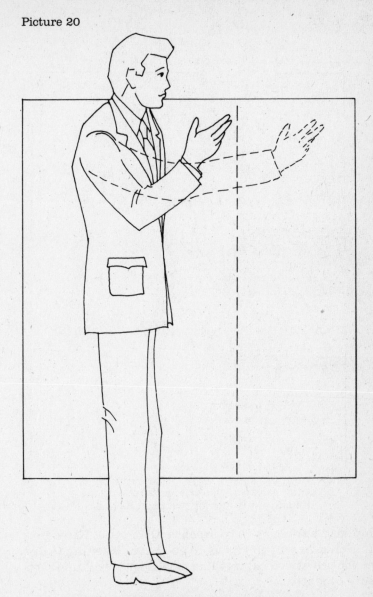

Standing salesperson's safe gesture territory.
Usually about 14 inches.

Picture 21

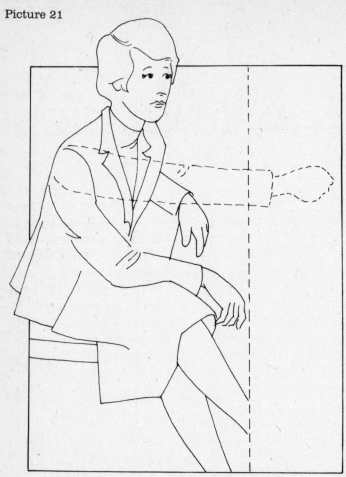

Sitting salesperson's safe gesture territory.
Usually ends inch or two past the knee.

ing may be doing you more harm than good. Rereading
this chapter will do you more good than listening to one
of the self-styled experts that this chapter will undoubt-
edly produce.

8

COMMUNICATION

If you can't communicate, you can't command. This was the consensus of 2,628 successful men and women we questioned throughout the United States—2,212 were executives in large and moderate-sized corporations and the remainder successful either in their own businesses or in fields outside the normal business spectrum such as the arts. Surprisingly, even though the corporate executive thought of communication as the most essential success skill, the men outside the corporate world were, if anything, more insistent that ability to communicate was the key to their success. In fact, one of the chief reasons they gave for their success was their ability to communicate effectively with their clients in large corporations.

The second point of agreement was that educational institutions, even those with very good reputations, do an abysmal job of training young people to communicate. The only disagreement is on the extent of the problem. One said that in three years she hadn't met a young man or young woman who could communicate, while another said that about 60 percent of the college graduates who came to work for her were adequate communicators. On average, two thirds of those interviewed agreed that 70 percent of the young people they met weren't able to communicate adequately. This included, in their opinion, graduates of major universities, including those with master's degrees and MBA's from some of the best schools in the country.

You cannot dismiss their charges as simple broadsides from the older generation. Their charges are very specific. The majority of these very successful people indicate that 60 to 70 percent of the people who join their corporation right out of an American university aren't able to write well-constructed business letters and that close to 80 or 90 percent of them need instruction on how to write a simple business report. One gentleman for whom I have a great deal of respect said that 90 percent of the business reports written by the people who were with his corporation for less than three years had to be rewritten before they could be presented to clients. This is in spite of the fact that his corporation pays very well and is able to attract the top graduates from the top schools.

While the majority of men and women in corporate America are convinced that young people coming out of the universities cannot write adequately, they admit that most of them eventually master basic writing skills and that they can be trained. The real problem for a substantial percentage of these executives is teaching young people to speak clearly. Most of them say that fewer than 20 percent of the people they work with are capable of giving a concise, clear oral report and that they have far greater difficulty training people to do this than to write a simple letter.

The men and women who run corporate America are so dismayed by the quality of our university graduates that several very large corporations have set up remedial courses for their up-and-coming young executives. Others have taken to sending their engineers and technical people back to universities to take liberal arts courses in the hope of improving their communication skills.

When I first started researching corporate communications I assumed that when executives complained about a lack of ability to communicate they meant that their subordinates couldn't write and speak clearly. Working on that assumption, I requested several corporate clients to send me a series of written reports produced by their people with comments on the quality of the report. I also asked them to send me video tapes of corporate meetings and to accompany the tapes with comments by the man in charge on the strengths and weaknesses as communicators of various people at the meetings. In an attempt to have a uniform measurement, we asked them to grade the reports of the people writing or speaking on an A, B, C, D, F basis with the marks having the same value they had in college, A being superior, B being above average, C being average, D being inadequate, and F being failure.

When we received the reports, we found the grades not only surprising but also confusing. There was very little, if any, correlation between the grades the executives gave to their subordinates and the ability of their subordinates to use language well or even accurately. It was apparent from this that when the executives spoke about communication, they were speaking about something other than the ability to handle language. Only in one third of the cases was poor language skills the dominant factor. In the other two thirds, the consensus among the researchers who read the reports and looked at video tapes was that the corporate executives were really commenting on the inability of their subordinates to present or sell ideas in an acceptable manner.

After spending nearly 600 research hours reading reports, looking at video tapes, and analyzing them, we set up interviews with sixty-two, or one third, of the executives who had sent us the original reports. We still had not analyzed the problem correctly. At this point we were looking into the possibility that the breakdown in communication was as much a fault of the executives as it was of the subordinates. We started by testing the listening and reading skills of the executives who had, in our opinion, inaccurately graded their subordinates. After doing so, the researchers believed that they understood what the subordinates were trying to say. We therefore started by testing the executives on their comprehension. We found that in 98 percent of the cases the executives understood the content of the report at least as well as our researchers. When they spoke of someone being an inadequate communicator, what they were really speaking about was that person's inability to sell ideas or the fact that the format the person used to report the ideas was, in their view, inappropriate.

The importance of the format surprised me. We found, for example, that in the same corporation engineers giving reports to different department heads were required to go about it in a totally different manner. One department head wanted every detail covered in the report. He wanted analyses of why the report was being done, complete background on the subject under discussion, and a review of the literature, and he expected the report to run twenty or thirty written pages. In addition, he wanted an oral presentation that covered almost every detail in the report. The man who ran the department right down the hall wanted just the opposite. He wanted short, comprehensive reports discussing only the elements that were new. He said he already knew what was going on in his department. He didn't need an analysis of the situation, and he didn't want any young engineer wasting his time. The reports that got an A in one department, got an F in another and vice versa. Therefore, the first rule for anyone giving a report is to ask those who requested the report what form they would like it to take. If it's a written one, ask for examples of written reports that they thought were good and possibly even examples of one or two they thought were poor. Then you can give them exactly what they want. Superiors usually will be happy to give you this information. If it's an oral report, the most critical question you must ask is, "How much time am I going to be allowed?" One of the key mistakes made by young people preparing a report for a meeting is to assume they will have the entire length of the meeting in which to deliver it. The fact that a meeting takes half an hour doesn't mean you're going to have half an hour. Ask exactly how much time you're going to be allowed and ask how much detail will be required. If the time is inadequate, state so before the report is given. This advice is so simple that many people may overlook it. However, if you remember only one part of this chapter, remember this.

The trickiest report to give is a technical one to nontechnical people. A key industry problem today is that everyone is a specialist—at least everyone seems to be. Both society and industry have become so complicated that the generalist is obsolete. All of who are technicians in our own field are now obliged to communicate our expertise to nontechnical people. The kind of writing that I do in this pop-science book is the most needed communication skill in industry today because often the people who are going to make judgments about your specialty, or about you, will not have an adequate technical background for doing so. Today's executive must package his technical information in a way that can be understood by nontechnical people.

Even if the people you're talking to are technicians themselves, there is often no overlap in fields. The engineer down the hallway who happens to be your boss may have only a limited knowledge of your specialty. If he is going to judge your work, you must find out exactly how much he knows before you report to him. The man in charge is often a generalist with an MBA, an accountant who came up through the finance section, or an attorney who believes that all points are debatable. You're going to have to package your information so that these people without any technical background can digest it. But simplify does not mean water down. You can never present your information in a way that will invalidate it. This is a very tricky procedure.

If you are assigned to give a report in your field, whether it's banking, finance, or engineering, to members of the general public or to members of a committee who are not experts in your field, you must keep several factors in mind. The questions that will occur to non-technical people are not the same questions that will occur to your co-workers, so you cannot test your report by reading it to another expert in the field or to someone else in the office. You are probably better off reading it to your wife, your children, or your neighbor, or, if need be, hiring someone to listen to you.

Before this book went to press, in fact before I handed it to a publisher, I hired six tenth graders with a B average to read the manuscript. I paid them to take a test and gave them bonuses for correct answers. After I analyzed the results, we discussed the book. The sections which they obviously had not fully grasped, I rewrote. Theirs is the base at which I'm aiming. These were intelligent young people who were capable of understanding rather complicated material if it's presented correctly. The first rule for those who write or speak about technical subjects is the KISS rule: Keep It Simple, Stupid! Don't try to impress people with your writing ability or dazzle them with your vocabulary or your technical knowledge. The essence of being brilliant is not making a simple subject complicated, it's making the complicated subject simple.

There is one other rule for people writing or speaking to those outside their field. Jargon is for jerks.

In our study of corporate communication the average grade on oral and on written reports was C, but the average grade for the combined report was D. The combined one is much more complicated. If you have to give such a report, there are certain basic rules. One, make sure that everyone has his own copy of the printed material. If they're looking over one another's shoulders, you will lose them. You can't speak to someone who's looking elsewhere. Two, make sure they're all facing in the same direction. If they're sitting at a long table, even if you have to ask the boss to move, you must speak from the head of the table. Everyone has to be able to look at you and at the report without turning in his chair. Three, every verbal-visual report should be written in the following form: the top sheet should be a highpoint sheet; under it you should have an outline of the report or a content sheet; beneath that, the report itself. It may have any of a dozen formats depending on the nature of the information. If your company has a mandatory form for reports that does not include a highpoint sheet, make one up and give it out with the report. If you can, place it physically on top.

The reason for placing the highpoint sheet on top is that you do not want people to open the report while you're speaking. You want them to be able to look at that highpoint sheet and follow what you're saying. The highpoint sheet should be an outline of your presentation. If you absolutely must ask people to read sections of the report, try to get them in and out as quickly as possible. For example, if they must open the report during your presentation to familiarize themselves with statistics or other written material that cannot be presented on a chart, your problem is to get them to open the report, look at the necessary section, and, when they're finished, to shut the report and place it face up on the table. There are several techniques you can use. The simplest technique is to say, "Gentlemen, go to page ninety-seven. When you're finished, shut the report so we know when everyone is ready to discuss this section." This forces someone who wants to continue reading to close his report because you're not going to say anything until everyone has indicated he is finished. Everyone will feel group pressure to close the report and rejoin you. Two, make sure that on page 97 you have only the information you want them to read. Even if you have to do some rather extraordinary juggling to do this, it is worth the effort. Three, if you have to have them go into the report several times to read one or two paragraphs and you don't want them reading the entire page, make sure the appropriate paragraphs are marked off or underlined. Then you can tell them, "Read the

underlined section on page sixty-two," and this will lead
them to do just that and stop when they're finished. The
one thing you cannot let them do is continue reading
the report and ignore you. If you find them doing that,
you must take control. You must say, "Gentlemen, please.
I must bring you back to page one. You can continue
reading the report later." Even if you're the youngest
man in the firm and you're talking to all the vice-
presidents, you must still be in charge. It is one of those
times when it's not only okay for you to be authoritative, it's expected.

Remember, when you give an oral report you're not
simply passing on information. If you were, you could
hand out a printed form. You are there to sell, to convince the people that your point of view is correct. If you
present your information in a deadpan manner, without
exuberance or belief, you will lose your audience. If you
let people interrupt you, you will lose your audience. If
you read a written report you will lose credibility and
your audience because there is a difference between the
way people speak and the way they write. If you stum-
ble or hesitate, you will lose authority and your audience. If you present complicated technical information
in a way that your audience cannot comprehend, you
will lose your audience. And if you lose your audience,
you are talking to yourself.

All speakers must remember that audiences have personalities and react as a group. They react not only to
what you say but also to how you say it. They not only
listen to you but they also look at you. If your expressions and your gestures do not match your message,
they will turn you off. Therefore, before you make a
presentation to an audience, you should first make it to
a mirror and then to family or friends. You should do it
over and over again until you have it down pat. This is
important. When we questioned successful businessmen
and women about presentations they made, most of them
indicated that these were critical crossroads in their

lives and careers. The importance of preparing for such presentations cannot be overemphasized.

No matter how well you know your subject, preparation is necessary. Never speak off the cuff.

There are only two types of preparations: notes or a speech outline and a fully prepared speech. If you know your subject better than anyone who is likely to be in your audience, you may use notes. If not, a written speech is preferable. If you hope or expect to get press coverage, hire a professional speech writer. As a former reporter I can tell you that amateurs are never quotable.

Remember that all the preparation in the world is of no use if you forget what you were going to say, and it happens to the best of us. You must therefore not only have notes or a text, you must also follow it even if you have memorized your speech. The point of having notes or a text is to keep you from getting lost. If you have to start flipping through your papers, you will look like a fool and the audience will disregard you.

If you choose to read your speech, it should be typed all in capitals and triple-spaced on legal-size paper as shown on pages 138 and 139.

Of course, the preparation of a speech goes far beyond the printed form or even the subject matter. You must tailor your presentation to your audience.

Before you can do that you must determine what type of audience you will be talking to. There are really only five types of audience: the intimate audience, the boardroom audience, the classroom audience, the small formal audience, and the large formal audience. Each one has different characteristics and each must be treated in a different way.

The intimate audience is one you can speak to in your normal conversational tone without the help of mechanical aids. Usually this limits the number of people to six or seven. When speaking to such a group there are several factors you must keep in mind. First, always position yourself so you can see everyone and everyone can see you without twisting or turning. Avoid sitting in the middle of a couch or in the middle of a group; always move to the end. Twisting and turning will make you look confused, weak, defensive, and will cut dramatically into your authority and credibility. There are two basic positioning tricks you can use. First, you can move back from the group slightly so that everyone faces you when you speak. Or you can raise your head above the rest of the group. If they're all seated on a couch and chairs, you can sit on an arm of the couch. When talking with such a group, remember that you are better off if the majority of the people agree with you. With intimate groups, whoever controls the majority controls the atmosphere for acceptance. If you've ever been the only Democrat at a meeting of Republicans, the only Republican at a meeting of Democrats, you know exactly what I mean. Never bring up an important topic when you think you're outnumbered in an intimate group.

The boardroom audience is a small group of fewer than fifteen people who cannot hear you when you use a conversational tone. Speaking to a boardroom audience, you have to either speak up or stand up. We would suggest you do both. With the boardroom or conference audience, however, you still maintain a friendly, if not conversational, tone. Do not start to preach and avoid exaggerated gestures. If you are going to give a report in a boardroom or conference room, and it must be given from your seat, you should attempt to sit at either end of the table. If you cannot sit in one of those positions, sit to the right of the person who's running the meeting. If you cannot get that seat, stand up and move to the upper-right position when speaking. If you need an excuse to stand there, bring in a chart and place it there before the meeting begins. Never speak from the middle of the table or from a seated position unless you have absolutely no choice.

The standard classroom setup is a group of seated people with a person standing on the same level and speaking without the aid of a microphone. The standard audiovisual aids used in this environment are charts, blackboard, and chalk. The style used is almost identical to that used in a boardroom setting, possibly with a little more emphasis and formality. You must use restrained gestures since the audience can see your face very clearly. You will be more effective if your verbal and nonverbal messages are kept on a personal level. The standard academic classroom, however, is not a very efficient communications forum. A far better arrangement is the horseshoe (see Picture 23). This form of classroom was researched not only by my organization but also by several *Fortune* 500 companies. We came to the same conclusion: the horseshoe gives the instructor a number of advantages. First, the instructor can choose to stand outside of the horseshoe and deliver an authoritative lecture. In this position he is a high-authority figure similar to a teacher in the traditional classroom. The instructor may also walk into the horseshoe and, by doing so, automatically make himself a part of the group and create a rapport with it. Our research indicates that once you step within the horseshoe, the number of questions you get from the audience will automatically double. The instructor may go one step further and have a chair placed on the invisible line that closes the horseshoe. He can not only walk in, but sit down, putting himself on a level with the audience and creating an even more intimate rapport. Skilled instructors move in and out of the horseshoe forcing the audience to respond differently from moment to moment. If at the beginning of his presentation, the speaker finds his audience too distant, he may move in. If, during the question period, they begin to debate his answers and he doesn't want a debate, he may stand up, walk back past the invisible line, and again take the authoritative position. Because of its great flexibility, I suggest that anyone speaking with fifteen to fifty people use the horseshoe format.

This text is marked to suit my speaking style and interpretation. Each speaker should mark his own text, novices with the help of a friend or coach.

I AM DELIGHTED TO BE HERE
THIS EVENING . . .

KEY: | indicate a breath   <u>ALL</u> for emphasis
     || full pause   === more emphasis
    ||| pause for emphasis   ≡ maximum emphasis

FOUR SCORE AND SEVEN YEARS AGO/OUR FATHERS BROUGHT FORTH ON THIS CONTINENT/A NEW NATION CONCEIVED IN LIBERTY/AND DEDICATED TO THE PROPOSITION THAT ALL MEN ARE CREATED EQUAL.//NOW WE ARE ENGAGED IN A GREAT CIVIL WAR/TESTING WHETHER THAT NATION, OR <u>ANY</u> NATION SO CONCEIVED/AND SO DEDICATED,/CAN LONG ENDURE./ WE ARE MET ON A GREAT BATTLEFIELD OF THAT WAR.// WE HAVE COME TO DEDICATE A PORTION OF THAT FIELD AS A FINAL RESTING PLACE FOR THOSE WHO HERE GAVE THEIR LIVES THAT THAT NATION MIGHT LIVE.

IT IS ALTOGETHER FITTING AND PROPER THAT WE SHOULD DO THIS./BUT,/IN A LARGER SENSE,/WE CANNOT <u>DEDICATE</u>/— WE CANNOT <u>CONSECRATE</u>—WE CANNOT <u>HALLOW</u>—THIS GROUND./ THE BRAVE MEN,/LIVING AND DEAD, WHO STRUGGLED HERE/ HAVE <u>CONSECRATED</u> IT/FAR ABOVE OUR POOR POWER TO ADD OR DETRACT.//THE WORLD WILL LITTLE NOTE/NOR LONG REMEMBER/WHAT WE SAY HERE,/BUT IT CAN NEVER FORGET WHAT THEY DID HERE.

IT IS ALTOGETHER FITTING AND PROPER THAT WE SHOULD DO THIS. BUT, IN A LARGER SENSE, WE CANNOT DEDICATE—WE CANNOT CONSECRATE—WE CANNOT HALLOW—THIS GROUND. THE BRAVE MEN, LIVING AND DEAD, WHO STRUGGLED HERE HAVE CONSECRATED IT FAR ABOVE OUR POOR POWER TO ADD OR DETRACT. THE WORLD WILL LITTLE NOTE NOR LONG REMEMBER WHAT WE SAY HERE, BUT IT CAN NEVER FORGET WHAT THEY DID HERE.

IT IS FOR US THE LIVING/RATHER/TO BE DEDICATED HERE TO THE UNFINISHED WORK/WHICH THEY WHO FOUGHT HERE/ HAVE THUS FAR SO NOBLY ADVANCED./IT IS RATHER FOR US/TO BE HERE DEDICATED TO THE GREAT TASK REMAINING BEFORE US—/THAT FROM THESE HONORED DEAD WE TAKE INCREASED DEVOTION/TO THAT CAUSE FOR WHICH THEY GAVE THE LAST FULL MEASURE OF DEVOTION—//THAT WE HERE HIGHLY RESOLVE THAT THESE DEAD SHALL NOT HAVE DIED IN VAIN//—THAT THIS NATION/UNDER GOD/SHALL HAVE A NEW BIRTH OF FREEDOM—/ AND THAT GOVERNMENT OF THE PEO-PLE, BY THE PEOPLE, FOR THE PEOPLE, SHALL NOT PERISH FROM THE EARTH.

Picture 22

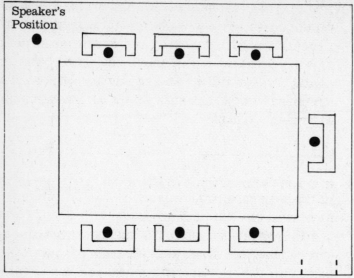

Boardroom.

The small audience is an audience in which anyone can easily see the speaker's face and read its expression. Speakers in front of small, formal audiences are usually on raised platforms and often behind podiums. With the small, formal audience, a clever speaker wears a lavalier mike, which gives him the option of standing behind the podium or moving out to the side. Moving from behind the podium breaks down a barrier between him and the audience. Before small, formal audiences, speakers are required to be slightly more effervescent and demonstrative than they are before a classroom audience. Once you are on a raised platform, the audience expects a more formal presentation. They expect exaggerated gestures, and they will not give you as much credibility if you do not use them. The same gestures and movements that would have seemed excessive in a boardroom are totally appropriate on the stage. Most businessmen, because they are used to speaking before boardroom groups, maintain their style on the stage. As

Picture 23

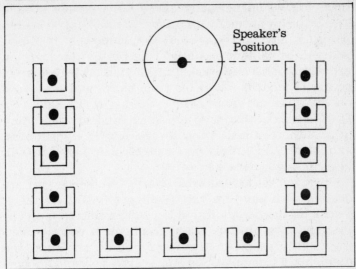

Horseshoe classroom.

a result, they are dull and boring. The minute you are
raised on a stage you must raise your voice when you
speak and you must raise your arms when you gesture.
You cannot talk to the audience as if you were talking
to a small group. Even though you have known the
people all your life, there is an expectation that once
you are on the stage you must be a bit of an actor. The
expectations increase by tenfold when you speak to a
large audience of 200 people or more. Once you step on
a stage before that many people you are an entertainer.
Whether you are running for the presidency of the United
States or you're talking about nuclear physics, your
first job is to keep your audience entertained. You cannot pass on useful information or convince them to vote
for you unless they want to listen to you. Large audiences have a personality all their own. They expect people on the stage to be entertaining. That is why good
speakers (almost) always tell jokes. But jokes are not
enough. You must entertain them with the subject mat-

ter. You must be exuberant. You must pause longer than you would normally pause for everyday speech. The restraint normally associated with executive speech patterns must be thrown out the window. If it is not, you will be another executive bore on the stage. If you are taking speech lessons, quit. Go and take a course in acting. The rules for using your hands and gesturing on the stage are more akin to acting in *Othello* or *On the Waterfront* than they are to giving a speech in any other format. Good speakers are actors, entertainers, and hams and unless you can become one, you will never be a good speaker.

Once you've decided what type of audience you are dealing with and how you're going to deal with them, decide on the mechanical aids you're going to use. The first and most obvious is a microphone. If you're speaking to fifty people or more and you do not know the room, insist on a mike. Sometimes extremely small rooms have dead spots, and without a mike, you'll be dead. You can always choose not to use it, but have a mike ready. Always keep your mouth at least six inches from the mike. Some mikes will pick you up even if you talk from the side, others will not; they are very directional and you must test this ahead of time. If you are not used to handling a mike, ask for a lavalier mike. These are small mikes that are hung around the neck or pinned to your tie or shirt and pick up perfectly at that distance. If you're going to be using charts or slides, wear a lavalier mike. It will free both your hands.

Use charts with groups of twenty-five people or fewer. When you have more than twenty-five people in the room, transfer your information to slides. The best slide projectors are carousel slide projectors and most hotels and companies have them. The only tray you should ever use is the eighty-slide tray. The larger one that carries more slides sticks too often. If you use slides, you must know ahead of time if you're going to have front or rear projection. Rear projection requires glass-mounted slides; regular slides will burn out. You can never put any printed material on a chart or a slide that you are not going to read to the audience because there is a percentage of people in the audience who will not be able to read it without your help. Extensive printed material on slides or charts infuriates audiences.

Naturally, if you're going to use slides, you need a slide projector. The rule for using slide and movie projectors, video cassettes, and other mechanical devices is based on Molloy's Law of Mechanical Devices. It states: if a machine can break down it will and it will do so at the most inappropriate moment. Therefore, you must be sure you have a backup item for each mechanical device you need. That means you need two of everything—slide projectors, movie projectors, whatever. If the person running the conference tells you that you really don't need a second one, that he has someone there who's an expert, pay no attention to him. Insist on a backup. You must also have backup for your presentation, a five-minute story that will fit in at any point in your speech when the entire system breaks down. And, of course, you must be prepared to go on without your audiovisual aids because there are times when it will just be impossible to fix them, even when you have a backup system.

Finally, the greatest breakdown in corporate communications that I've seen is communications between speakers and those who are setting up meetings. Do not believe hotels. They will promise you everything and leave you up the creek. If you are going to speak at a hotel, make a list of the audiovisual equipment you need and have someone in the hotel sign the list. In addition, be sure you have the name and telephone number of someone who will be available when you're going to speak, particularly if you're going to be speaking at night when there will be no one there to correct mistakes.

This entire chapter up to this point has been based on the premise that communication is message sending. But to a very large extent it is also message receiving.

All the great communicators that we witnessed at corporate meetings, and in person, have one thing in common: they are extremely sensitive people. The stereo-type of the American executive presented on televi-sion and in the movies as a hard, crass, unfeeling clown is untrue. He is a very discerning human being; that is one of the keys to his success. He is sensitive to every-one around him.

While watching the video tapes of corporate meetings we noticed that the executives in charge answered ques-tions differently depending on who asked them. We found that executives read between the lines—not the lines on paper but the lines on people's faces. They pick up very subtle messages. An executive in a major computer com-pany ran seven meetings for our video tape system. During two of these meetings he was confronted by his chief engineer, an argumentative man who insisted on his own way. In those first two meetings the man in charge, in no uncertain terms, said he was in charge and that was the end of that. The third time he was challenged, he didn't back off but simply walked around the question, said we'll come back to it later and very gently patted his adversary on the head. When we went back and asked him why, he said he sensed that the man was upset that day and didn't want to push him. When we talked to the man, we found that on that day he had been in a car accident on the way to work. Although this is a rather surprising example, it is not uncommon.

The men who run corporate America are great people-watchers. However, watching is not the main difference between the good and poor communicators. The great communicators are all listeners. They listen carefully, patiently, even kindly to their subordinates. They encour-age people to speak to them. They hardly ever step on a man's ego or a woman's sentence. Even if they don't like a suggestion, they treat it with respect and they treat the people coming to them with respect. The really great communicators are great receivers as well as great send-ers of messages.

9
POWER

My first job after college was as a management trainee for a large department store chain. I was immediately introduced to the company SOB and, unfortunately, spent my first three weeks working for him. To give the devil his due, he was a very efficient department head. He demanded, and got, first-class performance from the people who worked for him. His department was one of the most productive, efficient, and certainly one of the most profitable in the store. He kept it that way by intimidating everyone. One of his favorite targets was new young men so, naturally, he leaned very heavily on a friend and me.

Everyone in the store, at least those working under him, reacted to him in the same way; they respected him grudgingly, obeyed him fearfully, and hated him intensely.

After two months I decided to leave retailing for insurance. I put out my feelers while working for Mr. Charm and had received a couple of replies. Although I hadn't told my superior, I casually mentioned it to one or two of my co-workers. On the Friday I had chosen to hand in my resignation, a couple of friends and I were having lunch in the company cafeteria. One of the secretaries from the executive offices came in and gave us the bad news.

Mr. Charm was about to be put in charge of several departments and everyone there was going to be working for him, some of them permanently. The news elicited grumbles, curses, and a decision by three other trainees to quit the same afternoon. It only caused me to change my mind about giving two weeks' notice. I decided to leave then and there.

But as in most groups of equals, some are more equal than others. One of the management trainees apparently needed a lot less training for management than the rest of us. He was the only one who didn't talk about quitting. Instead, he sat for a while and listened and then suggested that if we all got together, we might get Mr. Charm instead of Mr. Charm getting us. He pointed out that since four of us were going to resign, resigning as a group might have greater impact. He went on to suggest that since I had already decided to resign before the bad news came and had nothing to lose, I would be the ideal person to carry the message.

I remember giving him a little grin because I knew I was being used and I wanted him to know I knew. Under different circumstances I might have objected vehemently, but in that instance, I didn't care. In fact, I liked the idea. Getting even with Mr. Charm would be a real pleasure. He had made a point of embarrassing me for no legitimate reason every day I worked for him.

Instead of resigning that afternoon, I arranged an appointment with the president of the company for Monday morning. When I got to his office I handed him my resignation along with those of my three co-workers and told him that I was quitting because of the man he had put in charge. There was no way he could talk me out of it but he might be able to convince the others to stay if he changed his mind about his selection for the new division head. I also pointed out that although there were six or seven other management trainees who had not handed in their resignations, from what I understood, they were looking around.

The president of the store gave me a speech about snotnoses interfering in management and told me I did not have to give him two weeks' notice but I could leave at the end of the day, which I did. He then proceeded to act as if my announcement had no impact at all. However, when I checked back three weeks later, I found that our friend was still running only one department instead of six and that another man had been given his promotion.

The most important thing you must know about power is how to use it and when to use it.

One year before writing this chapter I gave a two-day seminar based on our power research to forty-six young men and seventeen young women, all of whom had been identified by superiors as poor power players. Nine months later I contacted these same managers and asked if the course had been effective. They reported that the course had been extremely effective, that thirty-nine of the young men and fifteen of the young women had improved their power profiles. They were giving orders and, in some cases, for the first time, they were being carried out by their subordinates. Although admittedly none of them were as yet polished power-users, they were certainly more effective than they had been. More significantly, twenty-six of these young men and thirteen of these young women were now being considered for first-run management positions, whereas only nine months before all of them had been out of the running.

The report we received about the young women indicated that their improvement was far more dramatic than that of the men. Apparently, women in their normal socialization are not taught about power. Most of them had never played team sports in which they had to take charge, interact under pressure, or lead a group, which is where most young men learn to lead and to follow. As a result, the women had little or no practice in exercising authority. However, once they were taught the fundamentals, they exercised power with as much proficiency and know-how as any man.

The information in this chapter works. It will give anyone who reads it carefully a new weapon system. But before passing on the weapon, I would like to remind the reader that most men who have handled this weapon

have considered it a two-edged sword. Just about everyone who has been in power has come to realize its
dilemma sooner or later. The literature is full of quotes
about its dangers from those who have exercised power.
I have chosen two from opposite ends of the spectrum so
that the reader will understand how universal the fear
of power is by those who have wielded it. Jimmy Walker,
the very colorful mayor of New York, who sought power
for glamour, borrowed a quote from someone else when
he said, "Be nice to the people you meet on the way up,
because you are going to meet the same people on the
way down." Napoleon, who sought power for its own
sake, expressed exactly the same idea somewhat differently when he said, "Any leader who makes enemies of
people he meets while gaining his leadership is a fool
and will not be a leader long." If you read and believed
all those books and articles that suggest that the way to
the top is over the bodies of everyone you meet, you'd be
very wise to make a painful reappraisal of your present
work-style.

Nevertheless, most of the executives we questioned
said the main problem their subordinates had with power
wasn't that they overused it, but that they didn't know
how to use it. They agreed this was particularly true of
women. This fact was confirmed by the women executives we talked to, who stressed that the chief stumbling
block in most young women's careers is their inability
or unwillingness to use power. One woman, the vice-
president of a major marketing firm, phrased it rather
comically: "If you can't kick tail, you're gonna get your
tail kicked, particularly if you're a woman." The men we
questioned did not think that power is a sexual problem
but a universal one. The president of a large manufacturing company said, "If a man can't use power on those
occasions when he needs it to get the job done, he's not
going anywhere." The head of a marketing department
in a *Fortune* 500 company commented with a touch of
sarcasm, "In this company and in every other company,
in spite of all the fancy glass doors and the $400 suits,

there are those who are doing and those who are being done to. If you don't know how to play the game, you are going to fall into the latter category." The man who seemed to hit the nail on the head was an executive in a large computer company. He said, "If you can't get the people under you to do what you want them to do, even when they want to do something else, you don't belong in the executive suite and you probably won't get there."

In spite of their hard-boiled realism, most of the executives were very charming. The real killers are always charmers. They seldom use raw power in business. You know they have it, but you don't get the feeling the ax is about to fall on your neck. They relax you, they talk to you, they persuade you. Their main weapon is leadership, not raw force. They get people to want to do what they want them to do. Nevertheless, these very polished ladies and gentlemen said that this chapter is critical to a book on making it, because they recognize that their power of persuasion rests to a large degree upon the knowledge of the people being persuaded, that even if they don't go along willingly, they are going to go along anyway.

I know this flies in the face of most of the management courses being taught today. The majority of recent MBA's we interviewed were convinced that management by objective is the new pathway for business success. A percentage believed that business is being democratized too slowly, and when they get in they are going to let people set their own goals and through this they will achieve increased production and a wonderful new lifestyle. Actually, all of the new techniques in management are useful, but they work only when the man or woman in command is really in command. This was the unanimous opinion of every executive we questioned. Further, they agreed that sooner or later in all business persons' lives, they reach a point where they have to know how to exercise raw power. If they know, they succeed. If they don't, they fail—at that moment, and possibly forever.

Although power has been written about by almost everyone, data on the most critical aspects of the subject is extremely difficult to find. The psychological studies that I read were often so theoretical that they were useless. They were more often than not based on the premise that one management technique is superior to others, and they usually reflected the personal opinion of the author. Many of them were little more than essays couched in psychological and semiscientific terms. In the few places where hard data did exist, it dealt almost exclusively with men, and even then, much of the information was contradictory.

The studies we found most significant dealt with men wielding almost absolute power in limited environments: the presidents of corporations, the heads of countries, the owners of companies. They were people who made decisions that no one in their environment dared to question. When I first spoke to them, they started giving me the same information they gave to previous researchers. But when I told them that as president of my own corporation I now acted dramatically differently from the way I did before the corporation succeeded, and when I went on to explain that as a fellow power-user I did not for one moment believe what they were telling me, most of them immediately changed their stories. For example, just about all of them told previous researchers that the way to get ahead in their corporation was to stand up for what you believe in, defend your position, take a chance, be a gambler. If you have a problem, go directly to the top. That's what they wanted from the people who worked for them, being fully aware that communication is essential to the man at the top and that if he cuts himself off from the people under him and doesn't keep the lines of communication open, it will interfere with his ability to run a corporation. Therefore, they said their object was to keep the lines of communication open. At the same time, they admitted that when they were subordinates, they backed down often when they were right, they sidestepped certain subjects, and they didn't circumvent their bosses to get to the big boss as they were suggesting those under them do. Because if they had, and their boss found out, he would have cut their throats and they would have never made it to the top. In fact, they didn't act at all the way they were suggesting that their subordinates act.

They went on to state the obvious: often, if you win the battle, you lose the war and, with it, your career. Taking the ball and running with it is nice in theory, but in fact, you have to find out who has the ball and who is willing to run with you. They talked openly to me because before the interviews I not only signed non-disclosure agreements, I also showed them that in nineteen years of research I never betrayed a client's or a subject's confidence. One of the things that all readers must keep in mind when they see the statements of the great and powerful, is that people who are great and powerful know how to look out for themselves, they give researchers the information they want the researchers to have. They don't bother to talk about unpleasant or uncomplimentary facts. They are never going to mention that in order to get to the top, they had to kowtow on the way up. In order to get along, you've got to learn to go along, and they never said they lied to their bosses because they don't want their subordinates lying to them. Almost every man I spoke to at the head of a corporation told me that at one point in his career he worked for an idiot, and he looked out for that idiot in order to take care of himself. In short, he saved the idiot's career in order to save his own. The man who came closest to telling the unvarnished truth said, "The only systemized training for leadership I encountered was at West Point." He learned that in order to give orders, you had to take orders. He said that what it really comes to is that "you have to take a lot of bunk before you can give any bunk." The key to power is knowing when to back off. You have to know when to say, "Yes, sir," "I'm sorry, sir, I'll do it your way," because, according to all of the executives we questioned, unless you learn very quickly to bow to power, you are not going to have any. Power is given by the boss *above* to people the boss thinks are going to help him. If you keep that in mind, you'll have the real key to power.

The most surprising bit of information we uncovered was that the majority of executives agreed it was easier to exercise power at the top, than it was in the middle. They suggested that if I wished to help power-seekers I study the exercise of limited power, since the skill needed to exercise limited power is substantially different from that needed to exercise power at the top. The authoritarian positions that a top man can take will not work in the middle. Several of them suggested I look at people in their organizations, particularly those in beginning and middle management positions, who were handling power efficiently. I asked if I could also look at those who were handling it inefficiently, and when they agreed, we began our studies.

We attempted, under a variety of conditions, to observe men and women identified by their superiors as good and poor power players. First, we observed them during critical power situations, corporate meetings, giving reports, etc. We also sent our researchers to them in various guises. They identified themselves as clients, co-workers, subordinates, and superiors and noted the reaction of the successful and unsuccessful power players in social business activities. We noted with whom they went to lunch, where they went to lunch, whose company they sought and whose company they avoided, how they dressed, and so on.

We also enlisted the cooperation of several of our client corporations. They agreed to have a number of their executives report on inefficient and efficient power-users. We asked for reports in specific areas. We wanted a general description of each person involved, his job title, category, and power relationships. We wanted descriptions of their relationships with the people around them, both past and present. We also requested physical descrip-

tions of the people and their environments. We asked
them to supply us with pictures when they could, and
most of them did. Finally, we asked for a summary of
their command habits, how they gave orders to their
secretaries and other subordinates on a daily basis. We
asked for word-for-word playbacks when possible.

We also requested reports on critical challenges to
their authority. We asked the executives to make careful notes the first few days anyone was in a new job. We
wanted specific information. We wanted to know which
signals they sent off when they were challenged: their
voice quality, intonation, language, and sentence structure. Again, if possible, we wanted word-for-word playbacks. We also wanted to know the nonverbal signals
they sent out when they were challenged: where and
how they stood, sat, moved; how they used their heads,
hands, angles of their shoulders, their bodies; where
they placed their feet; anything and everything. We
asked that those making observations draw little pictures if possible and note the position and exact movement of specific parts of the body.

At the same time, we were conducting a survey of
communications with various corporations. As part of
that study, we had clients video tape corporate meetings. These tapes soon revealed that the corporate meetings were dramatic scenes of infighting. We decided at
that point to analyze certain sections of the tapes and
use them as part of the study of power.

The first fact we discovered about power is that it is a
way of life rather than a response to a particular situation. Power people have definite personality profiles.
They are private people who maintain psychological barriers between themselves and their co-workers, their
subordinates, and their superiors. Most of the people
around them know very little about their personal lives,
and power people do not volunteer any information.
They never allow themselves to be the butt of jokes, nor
do they allow others to impose on them, even in minor
ways. They will take offense if anyone takes even slight

advantage of them, particularly if it is done publicly. They understand that power is a habit and in all their relationships they maintain a power profile. This usually means they have little or no social relationships with their subordinates, even incidental ones. If they had been having lunch with the same four people for three years and they become an assistant department head, they stop those lunches and start lunching with the other assistant department heads. Not doing this is one of the main mistakes women make. They attempt to maintain former relationships even when their position is changed. When choosing who among their equals they should associate with, they choose very carefully. If they are real power players, they will never associate with a competitor. In offices where there are two obvious power players, each of them gathers around him little groups of friends. Power players always attempt to enlist the most able people and avoid anyone who is incompetent.

Their relationship with their subordinates is simple. In minor ways they continually reinforce their positions. Their actions identify them as the boss. Our video tape studies show that, particularly at the beginning of meetings, they give subordinates trivial assignments: "Move that chair over here, Tom." "Mary, please get me a cup of coffee." In their everyday relationships with subordinates, particularly women, men often establish themselves as father figures, kind but demanding, big daddy looking out for the small and helpless. Once this parent-child relationship is developed, there is no way the power player can be challenged, even on minor issues. These relationships are not necessarily unfriendly, nor do they always involve executive plotting. They are often products of personality types or male-female stereotyping. They are also often the basis for real friendships. A classic example is the relationship between Mary Tyler Moore and her boss, Lou Grant, on the TV show. As his assistant, she had no power or authority to challenge him, because he fathered her and allowed her no leeway.

During their entire time on the air she always referred to him as "Mr. Grant." The show's writers had excellent insight into power relationships.

Another favorite method for power players to remind subordinates that they are subordinates, is by judging them. They judge their work, the way they dress, how they stand, the kind of restaurants they frequent. They never relinquish their right to judge. That doesn't mean they're continually sniping at subordinates. On the contrary, power players are praisers. If you do an excellent job, they will pat you on the back in front of other people and you will feel great. This accomplishes two goals. It encourages you to work harder and it reinforces the relationship. They not only pat people on the back psychologically, they pat them physically. Power players constantly engage in physical activities that identify them as the dominant person in the relationship. They approach a secretary's desk and without asking permission, take something and start reading it. They do the same with subordinates. They often come up behind subordinates and look over their shoulders. When they do, they will usually comment positively and negatively on what they see. There is a judgmental quality to everything they do. Under certain circumstances they will often compliment subordinates on tasks that are relatively meaningless. Some of the better power players we witnessed even set up artificial goals and deadlines so that they could praise someone for reaching them and condemn them for not doing so. They spent much of their time establishing and reinforcing the command relationship.

The only time you can identify a great power-user is when he meets with a challenge. Poor power-users immediately go for the throat. They start World War III, they commit to unnecessary confrontations. Good power-users avoid confrontations. They get their way without a fight. They nibble away at their opponent. When an efficient power-user becomes a department head and finds out there are two or three people in the department who are likely to challenge him, he sets up small power confrontations, things that his subordinates are not going to argue about. He will go to a troublemaker's desk and tell him to come to his office immediately. After rushing him into his office, he will make him sit down and wait before giving him a meaningless assignment. When the subordinate is out to lunch, he will go to his desk, take the assignment from it, read it, correct it, and return it. It's all part of the power game.

Good power players play the same everywhere. They plan. The rules they apply in offices work equally well in schools and at home. We found teachers working in very rough schools who had few authority problems in their classrooms. Inevitably they were the ones who used their positions to advantage. They were not necessarily the biggest teachers or the loudest teachers or the toughest teachers. They were the ones who knew how to manipulate people. They never allowed direct confrontations with student troublemakers during the first few days of school. They made it a point to give assignments that everyone, including the troublemakers, were required to do—usually a simple assignment during class. Then they made it a point to judge, criticize, and assist the troublemakers, establishing their relationship as a teacher before any confrontation could take place. By helping the students, which was their job, they were establishing their authority in such a way that the student couldn't argue about it. Before confronting anyone who is likely to fight with you, it is sound advice to give that person several small orders where there is no real possibility of a confrontation developing. Once you have established a pattern, discipline problems are not likely to arise. In a survey of the parents of teen-agers we found that those who were good authority figures tended to establish their authority in minor ways. Parents who insist their children be in at reasonable hours, clean their rooms, and look decent before they leave the house, hardly ever had major authority problems. Mothers are particularly effective at this. Mothers who straighten their sons' ties, make sure their hair is combed, comment about their shoes not being shined, are really very effective authority figures. Parents who argue only over major issues almost always lose.

Our research also indicates that where an authority relationship is broken down, it can be re-established. The technique that seems to work best is for the authority figure to give a series of small, inoffensive commands, being careful to choose areas in which there will be no argument. The next step is for the authority figure to make minor territorial invasions: take things off a subordinate's desk, straighten your son's room, and so on. Subordinates are much more likely to obey orders after a series of minor, seemingly meaningless victories by the person in authority.

We tested this particular procedure in three different schools with half a dozen teachers who were having serious authority problems. With a few noted exceptions they were able to establish their authority over groups, if not over every individual within the group. We also had a great deal of success teaching these techniques to young executives who were having authority problems with other workers. My guess is that to re-establish parental authority would be trickier, would take much longer, and would be a much more difficult process. But the rules of power and authority operate the same in the home as they do in the office and the school, so similar techniques should work over a period of time.

The habits of powerful men and women can create significant difficulties for their subordinates. In a later chapter we will point out that one of the best ways to move up in a corporation is to find a powerful man and attach yourself to him. That way, you are likely to move up when he moves up. You must also understand that powerful men and women are going to impose on you. Throughout these relationships, you must maintain your dignity or they will lose respect for you. The path to power is across a tightrope. Most of the men we questioned were now at the top and said that at various stages in their careers they put up with what they considered abusive treatment because they had no choice. They advised that when you are not sure what to do, go along with your boss. They also insist that you must draw a line somewhere. Never let your boss make a fool of you in public. The president of one corporation told me that he had a boss who poked and punched subordinates all the time. He absolutely insisted that the boss not do that to him. He told his boss that being poked and punched drove him crazy and he couldn't stand it. He pointed it out, he didn't argue about it with him. He was careful to pick a time when his boss seemed to be in a good mood. As a result, he was made an exception to the punching and pushing and he maintained his dignity while others did not. The vice-president of another corporation told the same story with a different ending. He had a boss who shouted at people all the time. He insisted that the boss not shout at him and swears that this cost him his promotion. He spent eighteen months instead of twelve in personnel, and he feels that this is the primary reason he is not president of the company today.

These obviously contradictory tales, I am sure, leave the reader with a series of questions, and that is exactly where you should be. I want you to know there are no correct answers; no absolutely right or wrong ways to handle any situation. If you don't know which way to go, don't fret about it. Some of the most successful men in the country admitted that during their careers they had been in situations in which they had to close their eyes and pray that they were doing the right thing. Sometimes they won and sometimes they lost, and sometimes, as they were going about it, they didn't know whether they were winning or losing.

One fact they all agreed upon: if you work for a powerful man and you try to play power games with him, you are in all probability going to lose.

If your boss looks upon you as someone who will not support him, he is going to get rid of you. The executive of a major insurance company said it best, "The mutuality of interest, rather than manipulation, generally moves people up the corporate ladder and helps them succeed." The president of one of the top 100 corporations in America, certainly the most powerful man I interviewed for this book, and a man who is constantly being described in major business magazines as a corporate giant, gave me this quote. He said, "John, tell the young men and women out there that the most important thing they are going to have to do is bite their tongues and say, 'Yes, I made a mistake,' even when they are not sure. If they are not sure, duck when their boss swings. I had to eliminate two people from contention for top positions in the past few years because I found them playing silly games. Tell them not to come into a corporation with the idea of playing those games. Come in with the idea of cooperating with the people in charge. If that means acting like a pussycat, well, on occasion, they're going to have to do that, because if you take two men making ten decisions, they are going to disagree at least four or five times. Which means there will be constant fighting if no one is in charge. Occasionally, if you are a subordinate, you have to act like a pussycat, because that's the way the world works."

While you occasionally have to act like a pussycat with your superiors, apparently you should always be a tiger when dealing with your subordinates. Our research does not suggest that you always use an iron fist, but it does suggest that there be an iron fist in the velvet glove. Surveys of superiors, co-workers, and subordinates indicate that most employees are happier, more productive, and more effective when working for high-authority figures. This does not for one moment assume that the Draconian methods are always in order. All employees should not be treated identically. Different personality types require different management techniques. An employee who lives on rules and regulations and keeps saying ought and shall, will respond to well-structured sets of orders. At the same time, the man working next to him may be a self-motivated status seeker who will respond only to some democratization of management. The fact remains that both of these employees will be more effective and certainly happier working for someone they know is a decision maker and in charge. Unfortunately, many of the management courses put the cart before the horse. Teaching management techniques to people who don't understand the mechanism of power is very much like teaching strategy to someone who does not understand how weapons work. For this very simple reason, this chapter teaches you how power works rather than the theory of power.

In most social and business situations, having upper-middle-class speech patterns is absolutely essential to have a power image. It announces to those around you that you are a member of an elite group. Even though we found successful men in their own businesses who had obvious lower-middle-class speech patterns, they were effective only when dealing with others with lower-middle-class speech patterns or with young people. When they had to deal with people who used upper-middle-class speech patterns, they were noticeably ineffective.

The simple declarative sentence is the bedrock on which power language is built. It is a basic, bare bones language with few modifiers. Power people, although they use complicated sentence structure and a rather extensive vocabulary to prove they are upper-middle-class, avoid these structures during critical power situations. They also avoid modifiers that weaken their statements.

Our research indicates that women are four times more likely than men to modify their statements with weakening phrases. They often start sentences with such phrases as "I think" and "I believe." Both signal uncertainty. Another weakening female habit is asking for consensus, for example, "shouldn't we all," or "isn't this the right thing to do." These are actually not calls for consensus but a call for debate. Men, on the other hand, in the same situation are much more likely to say, "now that we have solved the problem, let's do X," or "now that we have eliminated the objection, let's do Y." Even when both are married to management by objective techniques, men and women handle consensus differently. Men are likely to seek consensus through direction. "Now that we have eliminated the objections let's go on and do 1, 2, 3." Women will seek consensus by question. "Don't you think we should be doing 1, 2, or 3?" And the consensus through questioning never arrives.

Power people not only use different vocabulary and sentence structure, they use their voices differently. Ninety-five percent of the men in America can increase their verbal power image by lowering their voices from a half to a full octave. Ninety-five percent of the women, on the other hand, can increase their verbal power image by dropping their voices a full octave and slowing them down a great deal. Most women, particularly when excited, speak much too rapidly and lose effectiveness as a result. A woman must take special caution never to raise her voice to a screech or a squeal level. Once she does she appears to have lost control and with it she loses her power. While a man can shout and scream to increase his power on a particular occasion, women almost never can do that effectively.

As we pointed out previously, power people are at their best during critical power situations. It means they use their best power voice as well as their most effective mannerisms. Men drop their voices the half octave and women drop their voices a full octave, when challenged. Some women who are consummate power players have true power voices as do some men. A power voice is not only slower, it has a different intonation. It is almost solemn. This solemnity is helpful to the power image of a man and absolutely critical to the power image of a woman. When we play the order-giving voices of some of the best women power figures without pictures, those listening describe their voices as steely, icy, precise, and distinct. However, if you are not a power figure in your environment, you cannot pull off that solemn tone. It works only if you precondition your audience to take you seriously. If you have not, you risk being laughable. Your verbal power image must match your nonverbal power image.

The men who run military academies will tell you that authority is as much nonverbal as verbal. The basic authority stance is almost military in nature: the shoulders squared, the head erect, the jaw muscles tight, the mouth closed and unsmiling, feet planted firmly on the floor, and eyes steady.

If a person sits down he sits in exactly the same manner. The head remains erect, the facial expression does not change, and the feet remain firmly planted on the floor. The military are taught to keep their head and eyes unmoving. This is critical for power. The entire look is one of control. The authority figure creates a certain sense of immobility. Powerful people, when they are making critical statements, usually move their lips very little, some actually whisper. Although there are exceptions, they tend to be rather stonefaced. This does not mean that they lack energy or that they are dull. On the contrary, their statements usually are very vibrant. The power of their statements comes from the pent-up power of a motionless body taut and ready to spring.

Powerful people's moves are orchestrated. They are very deliberate and know what they are doing. They move straight forward and back. They hardly ever sway and they never move from side to side. The most effective power players use the implements on their desk effortlessly. Pens, pencils, contracts, or pieces of paper become power props. They always seem to know where everything is. They do not have to break critical eye contact or move and lose their sense of immobility to find something. When we questioned two expert power players about this both of them said they memorized where everything on their desk was located. And they did so deliberately. They believe it gives their movements a smooth, flowing, unhurried look. This unhurried character of their movements gives the impression of being relaxed while the tautness in their face muscles gives the impression they're ready to spring. This is not something you can turn off and on. It takes a great deal of practice because there is no artificiality in their movements or in their voices. Power is essentially part of their personality. For this reason you cannot simply put on a power voice and copy the power movements in this book. Power takes practice. If you attempt to emulate the power body language I've just described only when you are challenged, it will probably hurt your image more than it will help. If you wish to do it successfully, you are going to have to buy a full-length mirror, sit in front of it, and carry on make-believe conversations and give make-believe orders hour after hour. It will work even better if you purchase a video tape machine, tape yourself, play it back, and criticize yourself very harshly. Our study indicates that the study of power is closer to learning golf or karate than it is to studying philosophy. You have to develop a good power reflex, not an intellectual grasp of the subject. I repeat, power takes practice. But there are elements of our study on power and authority that you can apply immediately. They deal with presence, props, position, and territory.

One of the essential elements of power is presence, which depends on size, weight, and positioning. If you are six feet five inches tall you have a greater sense of presence than someone five feet five inches. Years ago, a study was done that indicated there was a greater correlation between the success of students graduating from the MBA program at Harvard and their height than between their success and their grades. The reason is simple. Big men have a greater sense of presence and a greater sense of power. Therefore, it is to your advantage to add to your sense of presence. There is an entire series of techniques for doing this.

You can start by wearing what is commonly called serious clothing. Very dark suits, in charcoal-gray or navy-blue pinstripe, with white shirts or blouses and obviously expensive accessories will add to your psychological sense of power. You can further add to your sense of presence and power by sitting in a large chair

Picture 24

A. Man with hands on hips—power stance.
Woman with hands on hips—non-power stance.

B. Man with one hand on hip—power stance.
Woman with one hand on hip—non-power stance.

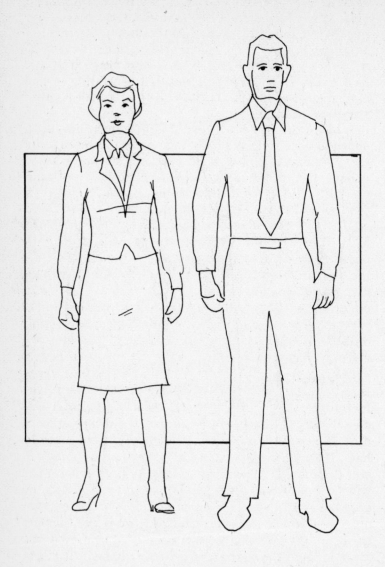

C. The most effective male and female power stance.
Straight, feet slightly spread, erect, almost military.

as long as the chair is not so large that it overwhelms you. One of the critical mistakes made by women who move into executive positions is that they sit their 120-pound frame in a chair that belonged to a 220-pound man. The enormous chair makes the 220-pound man look much more powerful, while it dwarfs the woman and makes her look like a little girl in her daddy's chair and obviously cuts into her effectiveness. If you take that chair and you put it behind a desk, you have again added to your weight and to your sense of presence and to your sense of power. If the desk and the chair have a window behind them or a series of pictures that frames the chair and gives it a throne effect, that too adds to the sense of power. If the chair behind your desk is set so that it is two or three inches higher than the chairs in front of the desk, you have changed the relative eye position of people in the room and you again, by changing your position, add to your sense of power. If you are a short woman you must make it a point to have your chair higher than the chairs of people sitting in front of you or they can come in and intimidate you in your office. You never want that to happen and naturally if it is your office your sense of territory adds to your power.

While some props add weight, others add status. There is a famous story of a stockbroker on Wall Street who had a picture of Rockefeller on his wall. He never told people that he knew Rockefeller but people assumed he did. He became very rich because his clients assumed he had information he didn't have. A very fancy and expensive desk is a more common status prop, as in an office with a view. All of these things add to your power and authority. In most large corporations the size of your office and your desk is determined by your position and there is little you can do to change it. However, if you are a young attorney in business for yourself, it might be wise to invest in a larger office and slightly larger desk if you expect to be giving advice to the rich and the powerful or to executives who have been conditioned to think that the size of your office is a reflection of your power.

Position is also a critical power factor. The person who has a superior position will often dominate the conversation. As we pointed out in the section on chairs, the position you should seek is an elevated one. If there is a stage, you can stand on it and sit on it. You automatically have an advantage. As someone who speaks 100 times a year to various groups and opens the floor to questions at the end of my presentation, I assure you that the kinds of questions I get and the way people accept my answers are dramatically different when I am on a raised platform from when I am on the same level as the audience. Height is not only power, it is also apparently credibility. So if you are at a meeting, stand up when you speak. At a long rectangular table, which you find in most conference rooms, the best position is at the head of the table farthest from the door. The second strongest position is on the right of the man at the head of the table. The third power position is at the other end of the table. You can not only add to your power by choosing the right chair, the way you position yourself in the chair will affect your apparent power. When you're seated either to the right or the left of the president of the company, if you angle your chair slightly away from him and face down as if you were joining him you reinforce your power image.

This position works because it associates you with the president. There is a whole series of nonverbal moves you can use to associate yourself with people in power. At corporate meetings we observed that most skilled power players sat as near the prime power person as possible, preferably to the right. When they could not sit there, they sat next to another power figure. The one exception to this rule is, of course, when the meetings are held in a subordinate's office. The polished power players will inevitably stand in the back and when they think the moment appropriate will start speaking from the back of the room and everyone will turn around and refocus on them. Presidents of companies and other top honchos are usually smart enough not to sit in front of a subordinate's desk. Even when seats are available they avoid them.

The final ingredient in power is territory. The territorial aspect of power is most effective when dealing with equals. Any powerful superior can intimidate an office-holder by purposefully invading his territory without permission. By walking up behind him, leaning over him, or even sitting on his desk, a superior can say he is in charge. He nonverbally says, "I have the right to invade your property. It is my sign of power. You are almost impotent." Beware if you invite a superior into your office. You may regret it. On the other hand, being in your office behind your desk gives you a definite advantage when you are dealing with equals. All the studies indicate that when equals gather, whoever owns the office owns the meeting.

I read in several books that when you are dealing with someone and you want him to back down, the best place to meet is in his office. This is true if only two people are present. He is more agreeable and easy to manipulate than he would be in your office. However, if there are other people present to witness his humiliation, he is far less likely to cave in. Because he is on his home ground he feels the psychological strength of territory. All animals, including the executive animal, will defend their territorial rights with tremendous vigor. Territory, however, is not just your desk, office, or home. It can be your restaurant or even your city—especially if during the meeting you pick the power position. If in your restaurant you are sitting with your back to the wall so the backs of those talking to you are exposed, you are in the power position. If you deal with someone who is very clever and refuses to meet you in your restaurant or your club or even to let you pick your own seat, you will have to meet him on neutral territory. However, if you show up at a neutral office with five people when the other party shows up with two, the neutral office becomes your territory because your people dominate the environment.

Your people can dominate the environment in several ways. The status of the people you bring with you or even their size can be a critical factor. If you arrive in almost any Washington office with your Congressman at your side, you automatically have more power than a man who shows up with his personal aide. There was an old-fashioned union leader in Chicago who insisted on negotiating with management in a neutral setting with two assistants. The corporate executives usually showed up with their accountant and lawyer. He ran a very tough union. He brought the two biggest, roughest-looking men in the organization. It was their job to sit there and intimidate the other side, which they did, and by doing so they made that neutral territory the union's.

Having a territorial advantage can be very useful. But you should remember that when you are in someone else's territory you have to be very careful. There are several best-selling books on the market that suggest that when you go into someone's office you throw your coat over his chair, spread your papers over his desk, and take over. We found these tactics counterproductive. We sent researchers into several dozen offices in which they followed the advice in the best-selling books. What happened most often was that the officeholders became very defensive or as mad as hell or both. If the researchers had been genuine businessmen and had had a deal with the men and women who owned the offices, those men and women would have killed the deal. The lesson is obvious. Being pushy and being powerful are not the same.

So I end this chapter with the same advice I gave at the beginning. Be careful how you use power. It's a two-edged sword.

10

OFFICE POLITICS

I talked to more than 2,000 executives about success and failure and only two of them ever used the term office politics. Both were women. Apparently, the term is not part of the lexicon of the male executive, but they did give a great deal of advice on the subject.

The first, most practical, and cynical piece of advice came from fellows who were friends of mine and as a result were being very frank. Their universal cry was: "Get yourself a rabbi." Now in business circles, getting yourself a rabbi has nothing to do with being Jewish. The term "rabbi" is used to describe someone on top who helps you when you're having a problem. Your rabbi is your mentor, your leader, and your guardian angel.

The term originated in Tammany Hall around the turn of the century. Between 1903 and 1918 a large number of Jewish immigrants arrived in groups from Russia and landed on the lower East Side of New York. The only thing they seemed to have in common was that each group was led by a rabbi. The rabbis were leaders because often they were the only person in the group with an education. As a result, their advice was sought not only on religious and personal matters, but on social and business matters as well.

When these men moved into a society run by Tammany Hall, it became obvious to them that if they were going to help their people, they had to deal with Tammany. Many of them became ward leaders and agreed to deliver so many votes in return for favors for members of their congregation. They negotiated for jobs in city government, admittance to schools, and so on. However, there was an equally large group of rabbis who, for a variety of reasons, would have no part of Tammany. As a result, one group of immigrants tended to do much better than the other.

The reason was Tammany's first rule. Tammany took care of those who took care of Tammany. It had only one other rule: if you wanted a favor from Tammany you went down to the club and you asked. The man who ran the club on the lower East Side in New York was an Irishman by the name of O'Brian who was a typical old-line Tammany boss, not very polite, but very effective. When someone who looked Jewish entered his club, before he'd get more than a foot in the door, O'Brian would yell: "Who's your rabbi?" If he gave him the name of one of the rabbis who was cooperating, O'Brian would invite him in and see what he could do for him. If the rabbi, however, wasn't on his list, he unceremoniously threw him out. Naturally, over a period of time he screamed "Who's your rabbi" at many people who weren't Jewish. But everyone soon got to know what the term meant. Instead of giving the name of a rabbi, they'd give the name of their Tammany connection. As a result, "Who's your rabbi?" became the question you asked people when you wanted to know if they knew anyone at the top.

The term and its original meaning were gradually picked up by men in business who still use it today. According to them, if you are going to spend your life working in corporate America, the first rule is the Tammany rule: get yourself the right rabbi.

I asked them the obvious question: what about the young people who want to do it on their own, consider having influence at the top an unfair advantage, and would rather not seek it? The majority said that that person wasn't likely to succeed, because he or she didn't deserve it, he or she was too stupid. The first rule of success is, if you have an edge, use it and if you don't have one, find one.

Since the best rabbis are blood rabbis, the executives we questioned universally advised that if you have an uncle, a cousin, or a father already in management in a firm, you attempt to join the same firm. They strongly recommended uncles and cousins with different last names because although nepotism is one of the key factors in corporate success, it is a taboo subject. You are absolutely forbidden to speak about it. Which means if you get a job from your uncle or cousin, mention it to no one. If your uncle or cousin is really important, everyone will know anyway. There is a second nepotism rule: never complain about nepotism in your company because you never know whose relative you're talking to. The reason for the second rule is that in about one third of the corporations in America being related to the right people is really the best way and in some outfits the only way to get ahead.

If you don't have a blood rabbi in a key position, use family friends or old school ties. These can be equally useful. Often men from one or two schools will dominate entire corporations and entire states. In some companies and industries, your religious or ethnic background can be a critical factor. A good rule of thumb is if 60 percent or more of the men who run a corporation or industry are members of an ethnic or religious group, don't go to work for that company or industry unless you're also a member of that group. If prejudice is not a factor, nepotism probably is; and where one starts and the other lets off is hard to pin down. If you don't take it into consideration when you join a company, if you think that all that is a thing of the past, you're kidding yourself.

Most of the people reading this book can do nothing about their families, their religion, or their schooling. It is behind them. This does not mean that you cannot have a rabbi. If you don't have a connection, you have to make one.

After you join a company, look around and choose a boss who looks as if he's moving up. Do more for him, produce for him; if you can, become his essential right arm. Work especially hard when he gives you a job. Be willing to work overtime and when he asks, travel to Paducah. Do everything you can to enhance his career. If you pick the right man, he's going to take up with him the people who helped him move. If you're one of them, you're on your way.

Upwardly mobile executives wish to gather around them coteries of younger people who will support them. The size and the number of people who want to work for you may be a factor in your upward mobility. In order to be upwardly mobile, you not only have to get a rabbi, you have to eventually become one. But before you can become one, you have to pick the right rabbi. If there are four assistant department heads and you become the protégé of the one who's never going to get promoted, you may end up being frozen under him. Therefore, you must pick very carefully.

There are several ways of spotting winners. In most companies you can immediately identify the people on their way up because everyone knows who they are. They're brilliant, hardworking, or connected. Spotting the brilliant and hardworking is fairly easy. Spotting the connected, although tricky, is possible. Before you make your move, before you join the team, find out who's who and who has the power. One of the best ways of doing this is to listen very carefully to office gossip. Get to know the office gossips and pump them. Find out who knows whom, who is related to whom, and who's been sleeping with whom. If there's a secretary who's been in the company for thirty years, she'll know where all the skeletons are buried. Get to know her. This information is critical. Unless you know who they are, you can't join the right team. Watch for little things. Take note of who lunches with whom, who drinks with whom. And if there's a young man who plays golf regularly with the vice-president of the company, don't dismiss it. Be very nice to him. The rule is: "Look before you latch on." Most of the executives we talked to said that the success books written today miss a very important point. In most cases, it's mutual interest rather than manipulation that helps people get ahead. You must recognize that other people in the company have interests in common. The minute you go into a management position, check very carefully on the people who work for you and the people on whom you're going to be reporting. Look at their personnel files, find out who got them the job, check their letters of recommendation very carefully. If you don't know the name of the person on the letter of recommendation, see if you can find out. As one partner in a major accounting firm said, "If you've got a young man working under you as an accountant who can't count past ten without taking off his shoes, and you find that one of the top partners in the firm wrote his letter of recommendation, you had better be very careful about what you write in his job appraisal. You are not going to recommend him for a top slot, but you are going to phrase his evaluation in such a way that they can read it any way they want." The minute you put in writing that that young man is the stupidest person in the company, he no longer is. You are.

Once you've settled into the corporation and decided who you wish to follow to the top, decided who your friends and allies are and who your potential enemies are, your job is to catch a rising star. And keep your enemy list as small as possible.

In order to attach yourself to a rising star, you should attempt to draw favorable attention to yourself. No matter who your rabbi is, you're better off if you can make your presence known to as many men at the top as possible. If they simply know your name, you have an advantage over someone they don't know. After all, on the occasions when they need someone quickly, the first name that pops into mind is the person they will use. The men and women we discussed this with said there is a whole variety of ways to go about getting yourself known. The first and simplest is that if someone compliments you for doing a wonderful job, tell him not to tell you but to tell your boss. And don't simply tell him, give him a practical way of going about this. Have the name and address of your boss readily available and suggest that he write a letter. You can point out to him that it's the only way your boss is going to know what you're doing and that you'd appreciate it. A lot of people will take your suggestion and send that all-important complimentary letter which will be put in your file.

If you can't get a key letter that way, try the trade-off system. Inevitably, you're going to have clients come to you who want you to do more for them than you do for everybody else. Your company normally performs services 1, 2, 3, and 4, but they're going to request that you do 1, 2, 3, 4, and 5. And they're going to request that you do 5 free. If you can possibly perform 5, do it. However, explain in great detail to these people that it is not standard company policy, that you're going out of your way, that you are going to spend Saturday doing it because it would be unfair for you to do it on company time. Since you're doing all this work, you'd appreciate it very much if they would let your boss know. You can give them a little song and dance about your boss not appreciating what a good job you're doing out in the field and ask them to write a factual letter simply restating what you've done for them and to thank your boss for it. If they're clever, and most people are, they'll very quickly get the message. One hand washes the other. You take care of me and I'll take care of you. That's a basic business technique.

Such a letter in your personnel file is extremely important. It can be critical to your chances of advancement. It is one of the best props you can have in that file and will do you more good at promotion time than almost anything else. If you can arrange for just two complimentary letters a year, you'll have an advantage over everyone who's doing just as good a job as you, and a few who are probably doing a better one but haven't documented it. If you've read as many personnel files as I have, you understand that many times the appraisals are written in such a way that you can read anything you want into them. The people writing the appraisals are trying not to commit themselves one way or another. They do a lot of fast footwork. Therefore, anything definite in the personnel file, positive or negative, weighs very heavily. Since in most companies clients and profits are the name of the game, a letter from a client is about the best thing you could have in your file. A negative letter, on the other hand, could be one of the worst things. So if a client says to you, "Unless you do X, I'm going to write to your boss and tell him what a bum you are," don't sit up on your high horse and ignore him. Do X, even if you don't think you should do X. Because that's really looking out for #1.

One of the men we questioned was head of the personnel department of a major firm. He said that even though he knew some of the letters he found in resumes were obviously arranged, he admired the people who had brains enough to arrange them and felt very comfortable in suggesting they be promoted.

Another way of drawing attention to your positive achievements is to do something that will catch the boss's attention. If you're a young attorney in an enormous law firm or if you're a young accountant in one of the big accounting firms, there is no way that the senior partners are going to notice you. You're just going to be one of many. You're going to be a number. However, in most companies, the people at the top have outside interests and activities in which you can participate, if you're clever enough to find out what they are. In one company we know, the president was the chief fund raiser for the United Fund. Everyone in that company went to work for the United Fund and attempted to raise as much money as possible. Because that's the one thing he saw them doing, he remembered. One very clever young woman I knew didn't go to work for the United Fund the first year she was there. What she did was go around and contact potential contributors. She spent a great deal of time lining them up, not just the month or two of the campaign but almost the entire year before it. The second year she joined, and with her earlier preparation easily outstripped everyone in the company. She stood out, and the president promoted her because the only thing the president knew about that young woman was that she did a fantastic job when he was watching. If you can become involved in the president's favorite activity—fund raising, charity, local Boys' Club, or anything else—it can be very helpful.

Being seen is very important. But knowing when you're being seen is just as important. In most companies, company meetings and company parties are known as "dog and pony shows." The whole purpose is to show off and to show what you can do. They are times for public display and they are critical to your career. They are often the only time people in charge will get to look at you.

When you attend a company meeting, don't treat it as a casual off-the-cuff thing. Remember, you're on display. Pretend you're at an interview. Dress in the same manner you would for an interview in your company. Conduct yourself as you would in an interview and watch very carefully what you're saying. Casual comments made at company meetings are made by fools. To quote one vice-president, "Anyone who makes a casual comment or a suggestion at a company meeting without several days' homework is probably making a mistake." Listen before you leap. If you talk before the boss has stated his position, you may find yourself in opposition to him which puts you in a no-win position. You either have to back off and look as if you're wishy-washy or you have to continue to oppose him. Opposing the boss is about the stupidest thing you can do.

When we looked at the tapes of company meetings, we discovered that not only did the clever people get on the right side of the boss's position, they also tended to get on the boss's right side. When their direct superior was attending a meeting, they sat as close to his right hand as possible. When he was sitting in the audience with them they sat at his right and when he was running the meeting they tried to sit in the front row to his left. It also became apparent that the people with power and prestige gathered together at meetings. In most cases you could psychologically join a clique by sitting very close to them. People made assumptions about associations that were not necessarily true. We also observed that the winners generally didn't show up late. They usually came in right behind their boss. They followed him to his seat and they sat themselves next to him. The people who popped into meetings at the last minute because they were so busy working and lounged against the back wall were generally losers. The winners planned their positioning.

We found that people who positioned themselves correctly at meetings had a far easier time speaking. The fact that they were sitting next to a man of power made it less likely that anyone would interrupt them. We ran a little test and found that if you spoke while sitting next to the boss, people were four times less likely to interrupt you than if you stood in the back of the room. When you do speak at a meeting, don't let anyone interrupt unless it's the boss. Continue your statement; do not be bulldozed. This is a particularly important rule for women. We found many of the women let themselves be run over at company meetings by men who simply interrupted them and pushed them out of the way verbally.

Remember, at company meetings you want to show

off your best, not your worst. If you have a problem in
your department, don't have a public discussion at the
company meeting. If possible, discuss your accomplishments. If someone brings up a problem in your department, attempt to have it put off. Suggest that you and
he have a private meeting. Tell him you can't discuss it
without documentation. Tell him anything, but have it
put off. What he's really doing is bringing the problem
to public attention and undercutting your image. One of
the rules at public meetings is defend your private
domain.

If someone brings up a subject that will affect you and
the people who work for you, be on your guard. The
standard defense is to ask the person who brought it up
to put it in writing so that you can give it careful
consideration. Never let yourself be forced to make a
decision in two seconds. The people who are making the
suggestion may have planned it for two months. If you
attempt to reply off the top of your head, you're working at a tremendous disadvantage. No matter how simple the suggestion or the comment may seem, ask time
to study it. Never let anyone run past you in this way.

And finally, remember company meetings do reflect
the attitude and the business philosophy of the men
who run them. Some company meetings are debating
societies because that's what the boss wants. In other
company meetings the boss sets up group A to fight
with group B and he sits there making decisions about
who's going to win. If that's what he wants, that's what
you've got to do. Do not try to change the nature of the
meeting. This will get you into serious trouble.

While most people recognize that their performance at
company meetings will impact their career, they under-
estimate the significance of company parties and company outings. These are also dog and pony shows. You're
being watched. The first rule of attending business-social
affairs is the same as the first rule for attending a
meeting. Dress well. Wear your best suit with a new

shirt and a new tie to the company party and upper-middle-class sportswear to the company outing. If you intend to play golf or tennis, don't show up in a thrown-together outfit. Invest in a good golf or tennis outfit from the most expensive store in town. More than half the executives we questioned indicated that it was very difficult to tell a person's background in the office. "After all, they all wear suits. But once you see them on the golf course, you really know what they're like." So the company party and the company outings are no place to let your hair down.

Just about every executive we talked to agreed that you don't party at the company party. In fact, after talking to them we were able to come up with a set of rules for attending company parties. Arrive when the winners arrive and leave when the winners leave. At most company parties the executives show up an hour to an hour and a half after the party has begun and they leave an hour or two later. Some even make shorter appearances. They're perfunctory in nature. They will have a private party elsewhere. They're not there to have a good time. They understand the function of a business-social meeting is mainly business. You must understand the same. The time of arrival is not as important as the time of departure. After the executives leave, the party usually deteriorates. It's about that time that the party is dominated by the mailroom or a similar group. Be sure you're not the star of the mailroom party.

When you walk into the room, look for the power groups. In most large rooms, the main power group will be found to your left just past the center of the room. The second power group will usually form a little past the center of the room to the right. If there are four power groups, they will tend to move close to the four corners but not up against them. Naturally, if there are buffet tables or other obstacles, the power groups will move to accommodate their physical surroundings. Take a look at who's talking to whom. Pay careful note of the people who seem to be very friendly, then pick a power

group and join it. If you don't know anyone in one of
the power groups, you have to make it a point to become
well-enough acquainted with at least one person in each
of those groups so that you can use him or her as
leverage to join the conversation at the next party.

I can't emphasize too strongly that you do not go to
office parties to enjoy yourself. You must act as if you're
being watched by someone without a sense of humor,
because you are. Companies have no sense of humor.
Limit yourself to two drinks and don't finish the second
one. If you're a woman, don't finish the first. Remember, you're not there to pick up the person in the next
department. You should not want to be known as the
life of the party, the person who does the soft shoe, or
plays the piano. The only thing you want to be known
as is an executive who showed up, carried on polite
conversation, and left.

If I sound like a wet blanket to the men, I'm sure I
sound even worse to the women. Women, particularly
young women, can damage their business image by
simply joining in what would be considered normal party
activities. I attended a party last Christmas at which a
very talented young woman with a great deal of potential was discoing. The movements she made on the floor
were totally acceptable for anyone who was twenty-four
and at a disco. Unfortunately, the people who observed
her were forty-five and had never been to a disco in
their lives. As a result of her dance, she became known
as the young chick with the build and the moves. When
I asked two women in executive positions how they
thought she impacted her career, one put it beautifully.
She said, "With those moves, she's never going to move
up."

The rules for women at office parties, unfair or not,
are much stricter than they are for men. I interviewed
twenty-six successful women and the majority believe
that office parties, specifically Christmas and New Year's
parties, tend to be traps for women. They agree that

many young women who act sensibly all year long make fools of themselves at these parties. And since it's the only time the people in charge really get a good look at them, they're making a serious mistake.

They also pointed out that this is the time when women executives are particularly vulnerable to traditional male chauvinist put-downs. As one woman said, for 364 days of the year a woman is treated as a competent attorney, topnotch accountant, and an efficient department head. But at the Christmas party, if she lets down even a little, she is apt to become "hi, honey," "a real cutey," "built like a brick house," and "a great dancer with nice moves." The first six women we interviewed were all in the same room at the same time, and every one of them had the same experience. They said that someone had tried the "hi, honey" technique as a put-down at a Christmas party. One told a very funny story. Five years before, she was working at corporate headquarters with six other women and thirty-five men. One of the men gave her a "hi, sweetie" routine at the Christmas party and she found out later that he had tried it with several of the other women. The women got together, discussed it, and decided he was doing a job on them and they wanted to get even. At the next party, they made him their sex symbol. They mentioned how cute he'd become and if he couldn't sell his brain he could sell his body. They kept walking up to him during the party and complimented him on his cute rear end and jabbed him. He left after three quarters of an hour. He knew very well that they were doing to him what he had attempted to do to them.

The rules for attending company outings are similar to those for attending office parties. You're not there to have a good time, even if you won a trip to Bermuda as a reward for being the most productive salesperson in your group. You can enjoy the pool, play golf, and participate in any normal resort activity. However, you can't drink too much, become the life of the party, and make a damn fool of yourself. If you want to use the situation in a positive way, you should attempt to join the power groups. There are power groups wherever business people gather. This time the power group will not be standing talking together, they'll be playing golf or tennis, sailing, or scuba diving. But they will be moving as a group.

Here again our research indicates there is a special set of rules for women. The women we talked to said that the clever ones avoid participating in sports that are male dominated. If they are able to compete in tennis or golf, they will. That someone beat them they thought inconsequential, if they played a halfway decent game. However, the women feel that they are put at a disadvantage when the men start playing softball or football. Most of the men were brought up playing these games and women tend to look inept and clumsy. When the women partook in this type of sports activity, the men relegated them to the position of poor, helpless woman, and that image was carried back to the office where they had to fight it. In the opinion of most of the successful women, it wasn't worth the effort.

The women I spoke to said if they were starting over again, they would learn to play tennis and golf. Several were actually taking lessons when I interviewed them. Two or three disagreed and said that participating in any sport where men had the advantage was stupid.

The final piece of advice offered by both male and female executives is when you lose, get out. They agreed one of the biggest mistakes made by men and women is not realizing that office politics is a deadly game. When you lose in most companies, you're dead and you have to move out in order to move up. They said the main reason for failure is getting in a rut and staying there. I realize at the writing of this book that we have a very tight economy and the nature of things being what they are, the economy may get tighter. When I mentioned this to many executives, they said that being an executive meant taking a gamble. You had to gamble on many things. One of the main things you had to gamble on was your own ability. They didn't suggest that anyone quit a job until he had another one, but they thought that if one out of every three executives started looking, they'd be improving their chances. Each of them knew of at least two or three men or women in their company, not going anywhere, who would have a possibility of moving up if they started fresh in a new company.

11

THE FRIENDSHIP NETWORK

Whether you get out or hang in you must get along. People who like people are the most successful people in the world.

The overwhelming majority of successful men and women we spoke to had a large network of friends. When we first started conducting these interviews, our main problem was getting suitable subjects. As a result, at the end of the interview we asked people if they knew of anyone else who would be willing to be interviewed and if they would recommend us. We found that when we were dealing with unsuccessful people, they only gave us one or two names and often struggled to find the telephone number or the address. They weren't good record keepers. Successful men and women were totally different. When we asked them if there were other people they could recommend, they buried us in names. They gave us names of other people working in the company and in the industry as well as neighbors, friends, people they had worked with five years ago, childhood friends, school chums, and relatives. Every successful person we asked offered us a shopping list of people from whom we could choose.

Two facts became obvious: one, successful people know a lot more key people; two, they name a lot more people from their past. Apparently, they keep up their contacts over a period of years. This alone would account for the fact that they have a tremendous network of friends. Since the average successful executive we talked to was forty-five and worked in at least five places before he reached his present position, if he made three friends in each place, we're talking about a man with fifteen very solid contacts. If, on the other hand, you move five times and the only people you are in touch with are the people you're presently dealing with, you have three contacts.

We found that in addition to staying in touch with their friends, successful people tended to do small favors for them. One man said that his attorney, his accountant, and his lawyer were all the sons of people he had known for years. It is evident to me that if he wanted a favor from any one of those men, he'd get it. Contrary to the popular myth that when men go up they forget those whom they knew in the past, successful men not only remember their friends from the past but they also take care of them. They do anything they can to help their careers and to put them in their debt.

I'm not suggesting for one second that most of these men and women have a conscious plan for making contacts, although I'm sure some of them did. Whether they were making contacts or friends is like asking which comes first, the chicken or the egg. I'm sure that some of them couldn't tell you because, frankly, successful people are always interested in contacts. Yet they have a real feeling of camaraderie and friendship for the people they work with now and those they worked with in the past. It's even possible they convince themselves that they get along best with those people who can be most helpful to them. But the end result is the same. When they need a favor or they need an edge, they've got it.

I witnessed a classic example of how that edge works at a convention in Chicago two years ago. I was hired by a company that does 20 percent of its sales at conventions to redesign their convention booth and sales presentation. I spent three days at the booth, the first day with three men, a young man of twenty-four and two men in their forties. One of the middle-aged men was the outgoing, gregarious type, the other was quiet and not very friendly. At the end of the first day, although I was more attracted to the outgoing man, if you had asked me I probably would have said the second was more likely to succeed because he spent more time with customers than with his competitors. However, I was sadly mistaken because the next day when I showed up they were all sitting around looking rather glum. They had heard the night before that their company had been bought by a large conglomerate. They were wondering if they were still going to be working at the end of the convention. The twenty-four-year-old took it rather nonchalantly as you'd expect. The two men in their forties were obviously upset. However, their reactions were quite different. The man who was very open and friendly with me apparently had been as open and friendly with other people at the convention and he went around talking to his friends and spent half the day out of the booth. When he came back at the end of the day he told us he had one job, a "maybe" on a second, and half a dozen other people looking for him.

The other gentleman sat there and said that he wished he knew as many people in business as the first. I found out they had both been in the business just about the same amount of time. The only difference is one made friends easily and kept them and the other one didn't.

When I interviewed executives about the friendship network, they agreed that it was important and constructive to have friends and keep them. However, many pointed out that it wasn't necessary to have friends. It wasn't necessary for a person to be your friend to do you good. Having contacts was often more important than having friends. One of the most successful men we interviewed said that in his entire life he had two or three people he could consider friends, but he literally had hundreds of contacts. He considered the contact someone with whom he was fairly well acquainted, someone whom he could call and ask for a small favor, ask for an introduction, or ask for a little piece of business and probably get it. He said that the reason these people were likely to give him something was that he was the kind of fellow who would give them something if the situation were reversed. He said that in his industry having contacts was at least as important as having friends, because he recognized the "know principle." They not only have to know you, they have to know what you do and where you do it. This is why the successful attorneys, accountants, and contractors we interviewed said they went to social affairs partially to make business contacts. They said you always feel more comfortable dealing with people you know, and so does everyone else. The more people who know you, the better.

Most successful people insisted that when they went to a party, they were there to have fun, to dance, to drink, to eat, to do everything everyone else did, but they always had in the back of their minds that they were there to make contacts. They introduced themselves to people and let people know what they did, even bragged a little about how good their firm was.

Frankly, I find myself doing the same thing. I sell what I do all the time. I talk about doing research constantly. I enjoy talking about what I do. I do go to parties to have fun and to enjoy myself and to socialize. And I'm there not necessarily to sell John Molloy's research. However, quite often that's exactly what I do. I believe that it is not a conscious plot as much as it is a by-product of being very interested in what you do and being able to talk and get other people interested in it also.

So, here's another way to give yourself an edge and a pleasant one. Make friends and contacts and keep in touch with both.

12
THE
EXECUTIVE SPOUSE

Well-meaning wives kill the careers of more promis-
ing executives than booze, bimbos, or social blunders.
We came by this information as a result of a survey of
226 American executives. The 192 men and 34 women
questioned came from 212 corporations and 23 industries and represent a fair cross section of American
executive opinion. All of them were management people
with at least five years' experience. As part of their
responsibilities, they groomed the future leaders in their
corporations and eliminated the losers from any shot at
an executive position.

These executives answered a three-part question. First,
we asked them why most young men and women in
corporations failed to get ahead. They gave all sorts of
answers. Poor attitude, lack of intelligence, and lack of
formal education led the list. We then asked what types
of mistakes were most likely to trip up a hardworking,
intelligent employee. Most of the 226 mentioned social
blunders of one type or another. When we asked them to
cite cases of careers that were short-circuited by a social
blunder, of the 611 examples recited, 326 of them dealt
not with the young man, but with his wife.

In 231 of the cases the wife was guilty of a sin that
theoretically does not exist in our democracy. She was

obviously lower class. Her dress, clothing, and speech pattern identified her and as such, she eliminated her husband from a shot at the executive suite. I will be the first to admit that this is unfair. However, it is nonetheless a fact. But since it is a fact that many women find understandably difficult to accept, I believe it would be worthwhile to let the men and women executives who made the accusations speak for themselves.

"Too much makeup, low-cut dress. You know what I mean."

"She was gaudy and overdone."

"Her jewelry and her dress look as if they were bought in the five and ten. Everyone at the table was embarrassed. She sat there in her $39.95 evening gown not saying a word, trying to be very proper. Of course she was obviously out of place. She knew it and everyone else did too."

"I asked my wife if she were wearing a cheap dress. My wife said no, it just made her look cheap."

"When I saw her coming in the room, she looked fine. But the minute she opened her mouth, *he* was dead."

"We knew right then and there that he wasn't going anywhere. Imagine an executive wife with bright-purple lipstick."

"Now, John, you come from New York and I can tell if I listen carefully. But my God, her accent was ridiculous! It was right out of a 1920s movie."

"Can you believe it? This fellow's wife was actually chewing gum and clicking it! I thought the president was going to fall over."

"She would have been all right if she'd kept her mouth shut. But when one of the women asked if she'd been to Bergdorf's lately, she said she didn't know the Bergdorfs and from there on in it went downhill."

"She's the only woman I ever saw eat with elbows on the table. It would have been amusing if it weren't so pathetic."

"They served us Beef Wellington and she used the knife and fork as if it were still alive."

"Our leading engineer had a problem. He married a woman that looked like a waitress in a cheap restaurant. It was our problem too. He was really a very good man, but we had to replace him."

"She talked so loud that everyone at our table could hear her. The president was so upset that he asked whose wife she was. Since we didn't know who she belonged to, he insisted we find out. The fellow obviously was not going anywhere. At least, he was not going anywhere where he represented our company."

And finally the man who seemed to sum it all up. "Her problem was that she was lower class. She looked it and she acted it. And of course, she didn't fit in."

The statistical fact is that 60 to 70 percent of women, no matter what their backgrounds, try to behave in a way that helps their husbands' careers. Unfortunately, they do just the opposite. It isn't that they don't care. Most of them care a great deal and try very hard. The problem is that they usually don't realize that they're doing anything wrong.

We were able to interview twenty-three women who had been identified as career-killers. Of the twenty-three, only one realized that she was doing her husband's career any damage. She correctly believed that her speech patterns hurt her image and she was taking diction lessons. The twenty-two others, however, had no idea of their harmful impact on their husbands' careers. Even the one woman who recognized her speech problem and was taking great pains to correct it, did not yet realize that the way she dressed was just as harmful to her and his image as her speech.

When wives kill their husbands' careers, it is usually a secret and silent death for a variety of reasons. If a man who repeatedly makes social business blunders is considered worth saving by his boss, depending on the blunder and the boss he will be told in different ways. The boss may come right out and tell him, "Look, fellow, you're wearing the wrong clothing. Get rid of that silly tie," or "You *must* wear a suit, shirt, and tie in this office." If the blunder is somewhat more delicate than a matter of dress, if, for example, he has poor table manners, the boss may tell him indirectly, perhaps through a series of hints. If the boss himself does not have the type of rapport with his employees that makes this possible, he might go to one of the man's co-workers or friends and ask them to bring the blunder to his attention. For the most part, if a valued employee of a major company is making a social blunder, there's a pretty good chance that sooner or later someone will tell him about it, directly or indirectly. Whether he's sophisticated enough to pick up (or accept) the message is another question. But he will be told.

But when a wife's appearance or lack of social poise gets in the way of a husband's career, no one says a word. There is almost a conspiracy of silence. Not one of the 226 executives we interviewed said they would ever think of telling a husband that his wife was preventing his promotion. Most indicated it simply wasn't a polite thing to do. One man admitted frankly that he was afraid he'd get punched in the nose. Another executive told of an employee in his department who was in exactly that position. The man was a good employee and the executive was afraid he'd take offense and quit if his wife's blunders were pointed out. The executive preferred to keep his silence and his employee.

The executives' reasons for not telling their employees are infinite and varied. But the fact remains, they don't tell. Therefore I suspect, and these executives confirmed, that there are thousands of women in America killing their husbands' careers without meaning to and without either of them ever knowing it.

Since no one else is ever going to tell you if you're one of these women, I devised a test that may help. We developed the questions after two sets of interviews. In the first set, we interviewed the wives of executives who had been identified as positive influences on their husbands' careers. We asked them to describe in detail their life-style. From their descriptions we developed twenty-eight questions with yes and no answers.

We then took the twenty-eight questions and combined them with seventy-two other questions that had been developed to identify other aspects of life-style. We gave the questionnaire to sixty-nine women, twenty-three identified as career-killers, twenty-three identified as positive influences on their husbands' careers, and twenty-three identified as women who neither helped nor hurt their husbands' careers.

As a result, we developed a sixteen-question test:

NO 1. I have upper-middle-class speech patterns. (Yes/No). (If you're not sure, check our speech chapter).

NO 2. I usually dress in an upper-middle-class style. (Yes/No). (If you're not sure, answer no.)

Yes 3. I am a college graduate. (Yes/No).

NO 4. I regularly meet with other executive wives on social occasions: bridge, golf, tennis, tea, etc. (Yes/No).

NO 5. I come from an upper-middle-class background. (Yes/No). (Upper-middle-class background means that your mother and father's friends were doctors, lawyers, or other executives.)

NO 6. I shop for my clothing in the same stores as the wives of my husband's co-workers. (Yes/No).

NO 7. I have had dinner at the home of at least two of my husband's co-workers within the last year and they have had dinner at my home. (Yes/No).

NO 8. My husband and I belong to the same country club as do most of his co-workers and some of his superiors. (Yes/No).

NO 9. I belong to the same social and charitable organizations as do the wives of other executives in my husband's company. (Yes/No).

10. When I meet a woman for the first time, I can tell immediately whether she is going to fit in with the other executives' wives. (Yes/No).

Yes

11. I immediately spot someone who has poor table manners. (Yes/No).

Yes

12. Although most of the homes in my area are in the same price category, I can immediately tell when I walk in the door whether the people who live there are professionals and executives. (Yes/No).

Yes

13. The women with whom I am most friendly are the wives of men who are executives or professionals. (Yes/No).

No

14. Although I am not an expert in my husband's field, I can intelligently discuss some of the problems faced by his company and his industry. (Yes/No).

No

15. Although I don't associate on a regular basis with the wives of the top executives, if I found myself at a party or an office gathering thrown into a group with them, I'd certainly feel at ease. (Yes/No).

No

16. I am aware of the fact that my background is not perfect for a woman in my position and as a result I've taken a whole series of self-improvement steps and believe that I've overcome my background. (Yes/No).

No

If you answer every question with no, it does not mean that you have killed or will in the future kill your husband's career. However, there is a definite statistical correlation between the number of negative answers and women who, in the past, have negatively impacted their husbands' careers. We found that the women who were positive influences on their husbands' careers very seldom had more than one or two no answers. We also discovered that those who were thought of as being neuter influences generally had three or four negative answers, but that they could have as many as five or six without greatly affecting their status. Finally, those who were identified as career-killers usually answered no to more than half of the questions. Our research also indicated that negative answers to questions 1 and 2 often put women into the career-killer category. These questions are more important than others because while the others measure life-style, these measure socioeconomic message sending. Therefore, if you answer question 1 no, you must take steps to improve your diction. Without upper-middle-class verbal patterns you will not create the proper impression. If you answer question 2 no, you should buy a copy of my *Woman's Dress for Success Book* and read very carefully the section on cross shopping.

Since we've given this test to several thousand women, I'm well aware that the immediate reaction of women who fail the test is to dismiss it as being inaccurate. They prefer to equate it with those quizzes they get in women's magazines that purport to rank their marriage or their sex life on a scale of 1 to 10. But this test has greater significance. We found that it accurately identified women who were positive influences on their husbands' careers approximately 70 percent of the time, and women who were negative influences on their husbands' careers approximately 60 percent of the time. I say approximately because whether a woman is positively impacting her husband's career is a matter of opinion. Nevertheless, if you answered all the questions positively, you should congratulate yourself. And if you answered more than half negatively, you should at least take a look at your life-style to see if anything needs correcting. It is likely that something does.

You can make negative answers positive if you make up your mind to conduct yourself in a different manner. Those that require some effort and some expertise are covered in other chapters in this book.

The answers to our questions revealed a variety of

ways by which women negatively impacted their husbands' careers. The blunder that cropped up most often was drinking too much. By the way, overdrinking at business or social functions is the main reason husbands kill their own careers. But there is a double standard for men and women. Men can do a lot more drinking than women can. As long as a man doesn't seem to be tipsy, he can usually get by. Women, on the other hand, don't have to get drunk or even tipsy to endanger their own image and their husbands' careers. In most cases, if a woman has more drinks than the man in charge (or his wife) thinks appropriate it will be noted and noted negatively. Our survey of executive men and their wives indicated that in any situation where drinks were served, almost no one thought that having one or two drinks was improper. However, if a woman drank more than two drinks her actions would immediately become suspect. If you ask yourself who's counting, you'd be surprised. If a woman becomes inebriated or simply seems to be, she can kill her husband's career in one night.

The same story was told time and time again, of the boss who had someone in mind for an important slot but canceled his ticket very quickly when he saw the man's wife drinking too much, or even looking as if she might drink too much. There's a particularly ironic story of a man losing his chance at a very important position because his wife entered the room, accepted a drink, said, "My God, I can sure use a martini," and proceeded to down it in two gulps. It so happened that his wife was a surgeon and may have had a very good reason for wanting that martini, but it killed his career nevertheless. After surveying several hundred executives and their wives, I came to the conclusion that the only absolutely safe rule for an executive's wife when it comes to drinking is: Don't do it at all! If you do, keep it to wine and keep it to two (the first one you complete and the second one you don't).

If this seems like too stringent a rule, it's not my rule, it's the rule of the people I've questioned. You must remember that many people were brought up in an environment in which drinking was considered immoral, and still others may have had very negative personal experience with alcohol, either in their family or their business life.

The classic example of a negative experience is the story of Champagne Mary. I was keynote speaker at a sales convention and was sitting at one end of the table with two people I had befriended. Looking down at the other end, I saw that there was a little party going on. Kiddingly, I turned to the couple I was sitting with and said, "Too bad I was stuck down here with the deadheads. I could have been over there partying with the fun group." They both gave me one of those strange knowing looks. After a judicious pause the wife told me that the young woman down at the fun end of the table was drinking with the vice-president's wife, but it was not a party. It was an execution. According to her we were watching yet another victim of Champagne Mary.

The vice-president's wife made it a point of not too gently pushing champagne on wives of the new men in her husband's department. Apparently at her husband's insistence, she tested to see if the young women could be cajoled or even bullied into drinking too much. It seems that several years before, the vice-president had had a chance to move into an executive vice-presidency at corporate headquarters, but his chances were tied up with getting a major account with a foreign country. He was sent to Washington to close the deal, and he took his chief engineer with him. The engineer brought his wife. The scope of the deal was so great that it required government cooperation. On the critical evening, they were invited to the embassy. It was understood that after the party, everyone would sit down and talk turkey.

The engineer's wife, however, dazzled by Washington's diplomatic finery, took a few too many sips of champagne and the engineer had to take her back to the hotel. The vice-president was left to attend his critical meeting without his engineer's technical advice, and consequently (so he believed) lost the contract—as well as his promotion. His wife, in her mind, was simply checking to see that the same thing wasn't going to happen again.

Nevertheless, I thought it was a cheap trick and I said so. But the gentleman I had befriended said, "It *is* a cheap trick. I don't like the man's wife and I don't like him. Neither of them are going anywhere in the company. But don't kid yourself. It's not that uncommon. Companies make a general practice of testing wives." When I started doing this research I found out he was dead right.

The most honest type of test is the invitation to a joint interview. In many cases, when a man is being considered for a position or even a new job with the company, both he and his wife are interviewed or invited for dinner or a weekend where they are closely observed. Frankly, the wife must pass muster with both the executive and his wife because the third most common reason for turning down a man is that his wife doesn't get along with the other women in the group. Many companies refer to themselves and their employees as family and take the description quite literally. These companies arrange it so that not only do their men work together, but they also play together. They believe that this creates loyalty and an esprit de corps. Under such a policy, if the woman does not fit in, her husband will not fit in.

Other companies are not quite as open and some do not even wait until the man is up for promotion before looking at his wife. They may send the couple an invitation to dinner or the club; or if it's out in the field, they may employ a second-rate spying system. It's standard practice for traveling executives to be obliged to visit the homes of their men. Often they will insist on being invited to dinner. If this occurs to anyone reading this book, you are not to assume the man is hungry and simply too cheap to buy a meal. He is probably visiting you because he has been told to check on you. His job is to find out if the husband *and* wife would be acceptable serving in an executive position. In all probability the company has been burned in the past when they invited a man who was an excellent field supervisor to take over a home office position. When he showed up with his wife, they wanted to shoot themselves. She was totally unacceptable, didn't fit in at all, created a lot of problems, and was, in short, a social embarrassment. As a result they decided that rather than eliminate the field people from consideration for top slots, they would send someone out to check on their wives ahead of time.

I know one man who had the job of spy in three separate companies and he said frankly it was probably just as easy to fill out a form. I asked him if he'd make up a form and what he came up with is as follows.

Question 1: "Are Mr. and Mrs. So-and-so gracious hosts?" This includes the wife's manners, speech patterns, dress, the way she decorates her home, the way she sets her table, the type of food she serves, the conversation, and so on.

Question 2: "Is Mr. and Mrs. So-and-so's home suitable for entertaining clients?" Again, this is a matter of personal opinion, but he indicated that almost everyone agreed that the home must be well decorated, neat, clean, and located in a fairly decent area.

The tricky part of the form, he said, would be the point of discussion. He was invariably asked questions when he returned to the home office about the wife's attitude toward her husband's moving. Obviously, the only way he could find this out was to bring it up in a pseudo-casual way. The answer he was looking for was, "Of course I'd be willing to move to help my husband's career! I'd be delighted to do so! Whoopee! I'd be glad to move." This indicated to him and to the others that at least she's willing to go along. The one thing they didn't want to do was move a man to corporate headquarters only to have his wife hate the move and give him a hard time at home every evening. This would make the man miserable and consequently an inefficient, unproductive worker.

The other subject of conversation that was mandated if his wife worked was "in the case of career conflicts [which the proposed move would incite], who's going to give up theirs?" The answer that the women's magazines offer in light of supposedly liberated company policies is *not* the one the spies are looking for. The answer they're looking for is that the wife is going to sacrifice her career for her husband's. They want wives to say, "Well of course I am interested in my job and I'm very dedicated to it. However, my husband is the main breadwinner and therefore I will go along with whatever furthers his career." In fact the very same companies that encourage career women to have full, meaningful lives and important careers make it a point to be sure that the men working for them are not married to such women—at least not the men who are headed for the top. This attitude is going to have to change. But the fact is that it hasn't happened yet.

The one element that I personally found offensive is the "Are you a dedicated husband and father" question. Our spy said he inevitably asked the wife how she felt about her husband missing birthdays, weekends, and anniversaries because of his work. If she, like a proud wife, indicated that no matter what happened he never missed such occasions, it would be a decided mark against him, because that's not the kind of man the company wants at corporate headquarters. The company wants a man who is willing to sacrifice his family for his career. Although wonderful husbands are to be sought by wives, they're not sought by corporate executives. He admitted, though, that in one case he had disregarded the wife's answer. He knew the fellow was a workaholic and was hardly ever home. He was one of the company's most dependable and hardworking field managers. However, the wife, thinking she was being supportive, declared that her husband was just about perfect and never missed a family gathering. The spy said had he not known the man personally, he might have believed the wife's declaration of her husband's preoccupation with his home and it would have killed the man's career.

However, the question that really threw me was the one about independent income. I have always thought that if I married someone really wealthy it would enhance my chances of working my way up in this world. Apparently that's not true. Companies do not want men whose wives have an independent income. Independent incomes make executives too independent. So if your wife buys a ticket on the sweepstakes and wins, don't let them print your name in the paper.

The final type of checking that my friend the traveling executive did was what he called the friends-and-relatives party. Either he or someone else in the company would strongly suggest that the man and his wife throw a little cocktail party while he was there. They should not go to any special effort, just a friendly gathering. What they really want you to do is invite your friends and neighbors over and bring him along. Let him feel a touch of home in a strange city. After all, he's going to be on the road a long time. If you believe that, you believe in Santa Claus. Actually, what he was doing at that point was not only checking on you but on your friends as well. The advice for this one is obvious. If you have neighbors known as Harry the Lush or Phil the Fighter, or after two drinks, Sarah the Stripper, don't invite them to one of these parties. I would suggest that you cultivate a few doctors and lawyers simply to have them available as potential guests. No two ways about it, this is a show and tell time.

All of these tests for wives are, of course, things that can be handled by any clever woman. She can get through and around them without ever actually believing in them, and many do. We interviewed sixty executive wives over the telephone. Fifty-two of them said they knew that they had been watched by the companies at various points in their husbands' careers; forty-three said they objected to it strenuously. Since there was nothing much they could do at the time, they went along and played the game, but if they ever had a chance to cut that company's throat, they certainly would.

So instead of creating that one big happy family which was the company's original goal, it created a great deal of antagonism in the executives' wives, which I'm sure was reflected in conversations with their husbands and others. I suggest that such companies are making a dreadful mistake by enforcing impractical standards on wives. Most executive wives realize the fact that they're required to entertain and most sensible women realize the fact that if a woman dresses improperly or speaks like a waitress in a bar, she won't fit into her husband's executive social/business environment. But beyond that, most women think that anything else the company requires is a blatant imposition and they resent it.

All of the women we interviewed indicated that they were also aware of one positive element in the scrutiny of their husbands, and that it cheered them in a way. It indicated, after all, that their husbands were being considered for bigger and better positions. They also, it would be of interest to note, pushed their husbands to ask for higher salaries. The general attitude was, "If I'm putting up with that garbage I might as well get paid for it."

When I asked them to give advice to the younger women, it fell into two separate categories. The first is how to beat the game. Most of their advice on that subject is reflected in this chapter. The second is on how to cultivate her image as an executive wife.

Executive wives have several problems. Many of the elements of their younger life-style simply do not suit their new, more affluent and prestigious one. They find that the jewelry, the china, the silver and the crystal, and even the furniture that they have is no longer appropriate to the life-style of a woman who's expected to entertain, if not in a lavish manner, at least in a very sophisticated one. To a young wife whose husband has his goal set on an executive position, the women I interviewed make the following suggestions.

First, instead of buying a complete set of relatively inexpensive china when you're in your twenties, buy one-, two-, or three-place settings of fine china. They suggest you buy open stock from a reliable company in a pattern that is at present selling well. You should take the same step for sterling silver and crystal.

Try to get your crystal first because a good glassware pattern is only on the market for approximately five years. They suggest that you then try to finish your china set because a good china pattern is on the market for ten years, and your silver last, since open stock silver has an average twenty-five-year life-span.

They suggest you buy these things from a good reliable store that has branches across the country and that you keep in contact with that store so that if the pattern is discontinued you will be able to complete your sets at a discount. If you do get a chance to complete a set at discount, they suggest that you buy extra pieces for those that might break or that you might need more of in time (cups, serving dishes, one or two extra-place settings).

They give basically the same advice about jewelry. If your husband gets onto an executive track, it seems that overnight you need a nice fur coat, good jewelry, and new china and crystal, and you just can't buy these things all at once. Instead of having your husband buy you a little ring for Christmas, a necklace for Valentine's Day, and possibly pearl earrings on your birthday, ask him to give you a token gift on two of the occasions and a very nice piece of jewelry on the third. Only by taking this approach over a period of years will you have the type of jewelry you're going to need for the life-style you're going to be required to step into "overnight."

The most productive piece of advice I received was from a woman whose husband had been the president of a very large corporation. She said that although her loyalty should be to the corporation her husband had run for years, it frankly wasn't. Her advice to young women is, "Remember, you spend an average of only twelve to twenty hours a year playing the damned silly games and the rest of the year living off of them." It's not that bad a trade.

While executive wives, at least to a degree, have reconciled themselves to the realities of American business, the same cannot be said of executive husbands. I interviewed several men who are married to successful women and found them to be a most uncomfortable group. Most of these men don't seem to know quite what is expected of them. They feel particularly out of place at their wives' business-related social gatherings. It is a feeling certainly not peculiar to men, but one that men are not used to. All of them, even those who are executives themselves, complained bitterly about the constant rumors indulged in at such gatherings. They complained that when the company people start talking shop, everybody else is out of the conversation. Husbands find themselves standing around like dummies or talking to their drinks. Paradoxically, when they are included in the conversation, they find themselves put on the spot. They're asked what they do for a living, and often they're asked in such a way as to imply that it is assumed they don't do anything at all. One Chicago lawyer has several versions of his own life story. One version gives the impression that his wife's job is a temporary one. In another version, he and his wife come off as equals, while his third version strongly implies he's simply a sex object living off her wages.

But not all of the husbands interviewed saw the possibilities for humor. Several mentioned that they objected to the Mr. Doris Day routine. They found themselves being treated as if they were their wife's property and not individuals. Here again they reflected traditionally female dissatisfactions. Women have been registering the same litany of complaints for decades. Now men are getting their taste of it and they really don't like this bitter sauce for the gander.

Most of these men were understandably interested in

their wives' careers and many of them had taken on such traditionally female duties as housecleaning and child rearing to give their wives the added time needed to pursue their careers. Nevertheless, the same men were so uptight about their positions that they almost always ended the interview when I mentioned the term executive husband. Executive spouse was a much more acceptable term to them. The very idea that their primary identification could be linked with their wives' careers and not their own was obviously too sore a point to even talk about. Even those whose wives gave them an A for attitude were visibly rattled by the suggestion that they spend half their free time being supportive of their wives.

These men were also reluctant to discuss what would happen if careers collided. The stories of talented women leaving the company just before they are to step into executive suites have become part of corporate folklore. Several male and female executives indicated to me that career collisions which often end women's careers are neither inevitable nor are they necessarily accidental.

Two male executives told identical stories about women in their companies. Both men had women employees who were about to be put into top positions. As soon as the promotion became real, both husbands suddenly announced that it was essential to their careers that they move and they handed their wives ultimatums. One husband, an executive in the same industry as his wife, registered a request for transfer when his wife came up for promotion. Then he informed her that he had no choice in the matter. A second was a doctor who gave up a well-established practice and moved to a community that was almost identical to the one he was leaving. What these men had in common was their fear that their wives were about to outrank them.

One of the executives admitted that he now would promote a woman only to her husband's level rather than to the level of her competence. He said that to do otherwise would wreck two careers. When we asked top

women executives about this, two attacked the policy
ferociously, three said it had some validity, and one
admitted it had happened to her.

There were exceptions to the rule. Several men said
that they would not promote women because of past
negative experience with wives whose careers had come
into conflict with their husbands'. But there were several others who said that if the woman was competent,
they didn't care if she was married to King Kong. If
she was valuable to them, they'd be willing to pay the
transport for his cage when she went on business trips.

The real problem with executive husbands, however,
is that they haven't got the foggiest idea what's expected
of them—and neither do their wives' companies. I cor-
nered twenty executives from eight corporations and
asked them to describe the ideal corporate husband.
What I got were twenty different descriptions. Of the
twenty, nineteen admitted that they had never really
thought about the problem before. One woman executive
pointed out that it is only another indication that corporations are still not really interested in women executives, which may be the truth.

Of the twenty I questioned, fourteen indicated that
while they hadn't given the matter of executive husbands much thought, a woman's mate could and often
would be a critical factor in her success. When pressed,
the executives questioned came up with a few characteristics that they thought would be essential for a good
executive husband.

Generally, they paralleled the requirements of executive wives. All agreed that he should have basic social
skills, though they weren't quite as particular about the
husband's social skills as they were about the wife's.
Also, they weren't as touchy about the husband's drinking at social business functions. More specifically, they
thought the husband should be able to carry on intelligent conversation, act as a gracious host, and dress in a
suitable manner.

Of the twenty, sixteen indicated that it would be an

advantage to have a prestige job. Further questioning uncovered some rather twisted reasoning. Even though the woman had succeeded on her own, these executives took into account her husband's position when measuring her prestige. The woman executive who was a doctor's wife outranked the woman executive who was a pharmacist's wife. And ironically, women executives who argued that this was unfair and sexist went along with it in practice.

The executives were consistent when I asked them to identify suitable jobs for the husbands of executive women. From the list I gave them, they chose only other professional and executive positions. But they also gave the benediction to out-of-work actors, free-lance writers, and artists. Apparently if you're a woman executive, you can support a guy if he's artsy-craftsy.

All twenty rejected plumbers as well as other well-paid blue-collar workers. However, if the plumber owned his own business, he rated much better. At first they maintained that they were rejecting men in these occupations for lack of social skills, but eighteen of the twenty went on to reject a man we described as a beautifully polished blue-collar worker. One said, "How would it look if our vice-president in charge of marketing was known as the plumber's wife?"

Frankly, all the executives agreed that it was only a matter of time until companies officially or unofficially interviewed executive husbands as they now interview executive wives. And they further agreed that a definition of a suitable executive husband would evolve in the same way it evolved for the suitable executive wife. No one knew what the final definition was going to be, but they were sure there would soon be one. I'm quite certain that not only the companies, but also the executive husbands would be happier once their role and relationship to their wife's company was defined.

Although women may not like the games required of an executive wife, the clever ones understand that it is a game. They can learn what the rules are as well as how to beat them. But executive husbands are in a constant quandary as to how to act, what to do, and what to say. Until their role is finally defined, they will tend literally to be the men in the middle.

13

AT TABLE

Even if Congress kills the business lunch, knowing how to play the restaurant game will be essential to any man or woman who wants to move up in business.

If you think that all tables in restaurants are by the kitchen door or next to the bar, in a draft or out in the middle of the floor, you don't know how to play the restaurant game. As a management consultant who is often forced to come up with a good table on short notice, I've learned a lot through trial and error. But I've also researched the problem for my column. I interviewed several restaurateurs, and executives who entertained regularly, and although the advice the restaurateurs gave did not always square with the advice given by the diners, here are some points that were agreed upon by just about everyone. Frequent at least one good restaurant often enough to be considered a regular. Get to know the names of the maître d' or headwaiter, a good waiter or waitress whose station includes the better tables, the bartender, and the owner. And make sure that they know your name.

This is particularly important if you're a woman. Women do not receive equal treatment in restaurants, not because the people who run them are male chauvinists but because women are notoriously lousy tippers. And since most of the people who work in restaurants earn the majority of their income from tips, they give very poor treatment to those who are known for undertipping. Therefore, if you're a woman, not only must you have a regular restaurant, but you must also show up often enough so that you establish a reputation as a woman who tips.

You must always make your reservation as far in advance as possible and be certain to specify the table or the section you prefer. You can do this not only in a restaurant where you're known, but also in any good restaurant. Even if you don't have a reservation, it's preferable to call a restaurant half an hour in advance of your arrival and ask for a good table. Particularly if you are a woman, you're much more likely to get a better table by telephone than you are in person.

Naturally, you must dress appropriately. Otherwise, even with a reservation you'll find yourself behind a pole or listening to the clatter of dishes. Most of the best restaurants, particularly in large cities, have a minimum dress requirement. They won't admit a man without a shirt and tie and even in those cities where good restaurants do not require shirts and ties, dressing up will help.

When on the island of Maui last year, we conducted a small experiment. We sent six groups of executives to different restaurants on four different nights. Three of the groups wore jackets. Most of them were wearing sports jackets, shirts, and ties, and a few wore suits. The others dressed very casually. The executives who wore jackets and ties found they were given better seats, better treatment, and more attention than the executives dressed in a casual manner. So the rule is, dress for better service.

A final point on which all agreed is timing. It is essential to a last-minute reservation. Keep in mind that most restaurants are packed between 12:15 and 1:15 and again between 7:15 and 8:30. There are obviously some local differences. New York tends to have a later lunch hour; Kansas City has an earlier dinner hour, and in Mexico City the dinner crowd hardly ever arrives before ten. If you avoid peak times in your area you can often get a good table even without a reservation.

One point on which restaurant people and regular diners seem to disagree is when to tip the maître d' or headwaiter. Restaurant people claim that the maître d' should be tipped after the meal, while most experienced diners insist it's more effective if you tip him before service. When we went back to the restaurateurs and repeated what the diners had told us, one of the men who owns a very famous restaurant in New York pointed out that the maître d' cannot seat you at a fine table after you've slipped him money in front of everyone in the restaurant. The other customers who may not be as well located will think this is the only way to get a good table and would take their business elsewhere. I believe the disagreement is not about when to tip, but how to tip. You should take into consideration the politics of the situation and be discreet. The ideal way to tip the person who is to seat you is to do it beforehand but not publicly. If you're unable to arrange that, you can assure him through various not-too-subtle hints that you will tip generously at the end of the meal. The best way, of course, is to show up an hour beforehand or the day before and tell him you need a good table for a specific occasion and slip him an appropriate sum. That way no one's embarrassed and you are guaranteed a good table. When you can't get there ahead of time, there are several ways to let a maître d' know, even in a strange restaurant, that you're used to finer service and you're going to pay for it. The manager of one of New York's restaurants suggests that you order a drink at the bar and tip the bartender a couple of dollars. Treat the bartender like an old friend and ask him confidentially to see what he can do for you. Chances are he will tell the maître d' there's a big spender at the bar who wants a nice table. Another ploy is, if you're waiting in line for a table, ask the waiter to get you a pack of cigarettes and give him a handsome tip for doing it. This will announce your generosity.

Another approach to getting a good table is recommended by a great number of people. It is the method of the masters. They operate on the premise that the headwaiters are there not to be intimidating, but to serve and to be intimidated. Here's the scenario. A master gets the name of the maître d' from the hatcheck girl or bartender. Then he walks up to the maître d' and says, "Charles, I must have a good table tonight." Now Charles knows he can't remember every important customer and this customer looks and acts important. So Charles doesn't dare take a chance of insulting such an impressive character and coughs up a good table. This is the type of advice that's given in most books on how to beat the restaurant game and it has a certain validity. But there's a word of caution that must be added. If you fail to carry it off properly, you will not just be seated next to the kitchen door; the indignant maître d' whose honor and professionalism you've offended will probably seat you in the kitchen next to, or if he can arrange it, in, the oven.

As important as it is to get a good seat in a restaurant, it is equally important to know what to do once you have the table.

As a host you have responsibilities. You should recommend dishes if you know the restaurant. After everyone has his menu you can make your suggestions. If you're new to the restaurant yourself, simply order for yourself and let everyone else do the same. As the host or hostess you will probably be expected to order the wine. If you know something about wines and foods, ordering is a simple matter. If you don't know how to order wine, ask for a wine list which is brought either by a waiter or sommelier. Whoever brings the wine list is expected to know something about the wines. Ask him for his recommendation and take it. This is an easy way out and relieves you of responsibility.

When the wine is served, you will be presented with the cork. It is not necessary to sniff it. Simply touch the part that's been in the bottle with your finger. If it looks undamaged, in all probability air has not seeped in and the wine has not soured. If it looks as if it has been damaged, smell the cork to determine any telltale odor of vinegar. The final test for a wine is in a glass. The waiter will proceed to pour a small portion into your glass. Sip it. If the wine has definitely turned, you can send it back. You should not send back a bottle of wine simply because you do not like it. If you're not used to tasting wine, sending it back is very dangerous. The restaurant may object and they may be correct and make you look like a fool. There are only two reasons for turning wines back: (1) they have turned to vinegar, and (2) the bottle has already been opened in the kitchen.

The rules for eating at a restaurant are almost the same as for eating in someone's home. Of course in a restaurant you have an advantage. The utensils are always set up so that you work your way in from the outside. You don't have to worry, the waiters will guide you. But if you do need that guidance, you're in trouble if you eat at your boss's home or invite him to yours.

Probably the most meaningful thing I can do to impress upon you the importance of table manners is to report a simple survey we conducted. When we looked at the men who were presidents, vice-presidents, and chairmen of the boards of major corporations, we found 80 percent of them had impeccable table manners. Their movements at the table were polished and self-assured. When we looked at people in middle management, the number with such polish dropped to 40 percent. When we looked at young people just out of school, the number slipped to 12 percent.

Even more significant is a survey we did of management people and their reaction to those who displayed poor table manners. We found that top executives considered it an almost immediate turnoff. About 60 percent of them said they would not consider letting an employee represent their company publicly unless that person knew how to handle himself at the table. They made no bones about it. They didn't apologize for it.

Picture 25

Standard place setting.

They simply made a statement. The possession of good table manners is an absolute requirement for any executive position in their corporation.

If you were not brought up in an environment in which your mother or grandmother or someone else taught you which knife and fork to use, I would suggest that you read this chapter very carefully. And when you finish reading it, I would suggest that you practice at every meal for at least two months. If you do not own the proper table settings, go out and purchase them. You have to have all the pieces to play the game.

Since the best place to begin is at the beginning, and each stage of a meal has its own set of rules, we'll start with the obvious. You sit only after the hostess has been seated and put your napkin on your lap after the hostess has put hers on her lap. After she has been served and has picked up her fork, you pick up yours. That is the signal to begin the meal. In short, at the beginning of the meal you play follow the hostess. When you start, the first utensil she picks up is the one that you pick up.

Picture 26

Variation on standard place setting.

After that, however, you may not be able to follow her because she may be doing other things, so you're going to have to know something about place settings. Since in some cases a picture is worth a thousand words, we've shown four place settings. If you look at Picture 25, you'll see the standard place setting for most American meals.

The spoon used in the first course is the soup spoon. The second course is the meat course. In this, as in most settings, you use the largest fork and the largest knife for the meat course.

The third setting is for the salad course. The dessert utensils are usually placed above the plate in the manner shown. There is no number on the butter spreader, as you use it whenever you like. The only thing you must know about the butter spreader is you never use it to cut bread. Its purpose is to spread. Break the bread or the rolls with your hands. The two other utensils at this place setting are a water glass and a wine glass. The water glass is the larger one. There are also individual

Picture 27

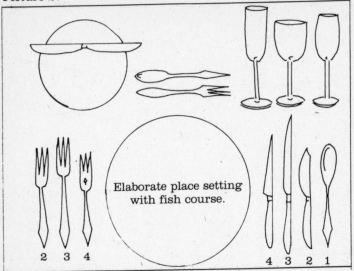

Elaborate place setting
with fish course.

2   3   4   4   3   2   1

salt and pepper shakers. At a large table, one set of salt
and pepper shakers is usually placed between two people or one is set at each place setting.

The second illustration (26) shows a variation on the
basic place setting. Here the first setting is for shrimp
cocktail, a traditional appetizer. The fork is known as a
cocktail or oyster fork and it is used to spear things. It
is never used with the fish course. The second knife and
fork are salad settings, placed here before the meat
course because the hostess may choose to alter the order
of courses. The knife is optional and usually used only
if cheese is served with the salad. Next we have the
third course which in this case is the meat course. Again,
the largest knife and the largest fork at the table are
used. Finally, we have a dessert course. All dessert
settings do not necessarily use spoons and forks. You
may also be given a knife, depending on what's being
served.

The third illustration (27) shows a more complicated

Picture 28

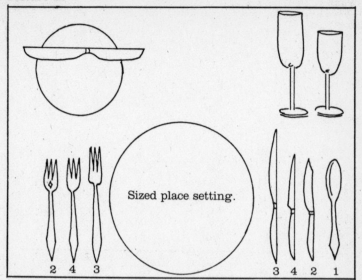

Sized place setting.

2　4　3　　　　　　　3　4　2　1

arrangement. This setting includes a fish course. The first course again is a soup with a soup spoon. The second course is a fish course. There are two ways to tell whether the setting is for a fish, dessert, or salad course. The knife for the fish course often has two little indentations on the blade and is a little bit broader than the one used for dessert. However, you may not know for sure until the course is served. In many modern table settings, the utensils used for the fish course are interchangeable with those used for the salad and dessert courses. If you simply obey the rule of working your way in from the outside, you're likely to be safe and correct.

Another way of spotting whether there's going to be a fish course is to notice the number of wine glasses that are going to be used. If there's a light tulip-shaped wine glass (number three) and it is a very formal meal, it is likely that there will be a fish course. The next course is a meat setting, again using the largest knife and fork. And lastly, we have the salad setting.

Picture 29

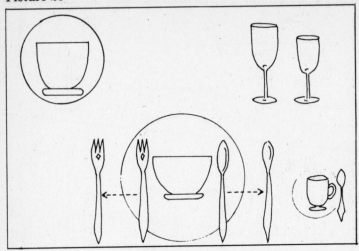

Dessert setting.

Picture 30

Correct use of soup spoon.

The dessert utensils at some very formal affairs where the hostess has an ample amount of help will not be placed on the table, as it would tend to overload it. They will be delivered after the meal as shown in Picture 29.

Picture 31

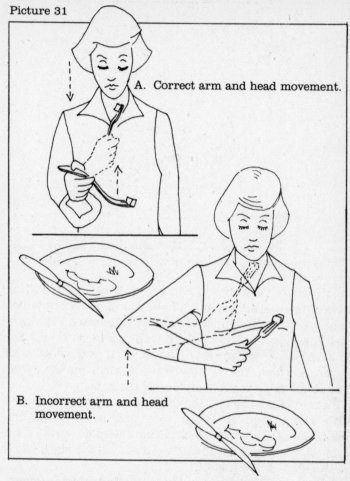

A. Correct arm and head movement.

B. Incorrect arm and head movement.

Picture 28 shows a type of setting that I think is incorrect, but that you may very well encounter. Any hostess who places her utensils in order of size runs the risk of creating a problem for her guests. Almost any hostess will place the soup spoon or the appetizer fork at the extreme right. After that the settings are lined up: fish, salad, and meat. Whereas the order of the actual courses is: fish, meat, and salad. As you can see,

Picture 32

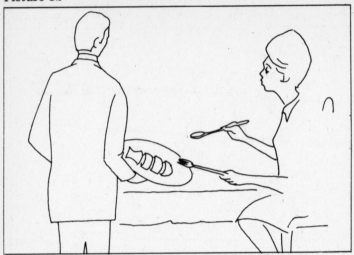

Serving yourself correctly from the serving plate.

the numbers vary. If you run across this type of setting where the utensils are not laid out in the order in which they are going to be used, don't get flustered. The general rule when dealing with a fish course is to take the smallest knife and fork on the table. If you're not sure which is which, fake it. If it's that confusing, everyone else at the table is probably doing the same.

Picture 29 shows you the dessert plate being delivered with utensils on it. When they are delivered on the plate, simply remove them from the plate and place them in their correct position (spoon on the right, fork on the left) on the table.

Obey the rule of common sense. If the dessert is gooey, use the spoon. Where you need to, use a fork. And naturally, you may use a combination of utensils whenever you find it necessary. If a finger bowl, which is a rarity today, is brought, it will be placed in the upper left of your table area.

Not matter what you are eating, use your utensils in a manner that will reduce the chances of dropping any-

Picture 33

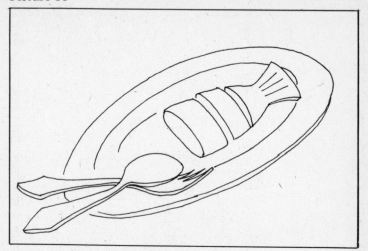

Returning utensils to serving platter.

thing on the tablecloth or on yourself. If you're eating soup, take the soup spoon the way it is shown in Picture 30, dip it into the soup in a motion away from you, and then bring it back to your mouth. When you bring it to your mouth, lean slightly forward. Don't go to extremes and look as if you're diving into your soup dish.

The general rule when you're eating is not to move the entire arm. A more sophisticated movement of the wrist with as little arm movement as possible is very important. Almost everyone will judge your socioeconomic background on how much you move your arm when you eat. Very limited, precise movements at the table are a sign of breeding (Picture 31).

During most formal dinners those serving you will bring serving dishes to you and you will be expected to take utensils from the serving dish and use them to transport portions to your plate. Take moderate portions. Serving platters always should be offered from the left side. Take the serving fork in your left hand and the serving spoon in your right. Hold them as shown in

Picture 34

Continental use of fork—left hand, prongs down.

Picture 35

American use of fork—right hand, prongs up.

Picture 36

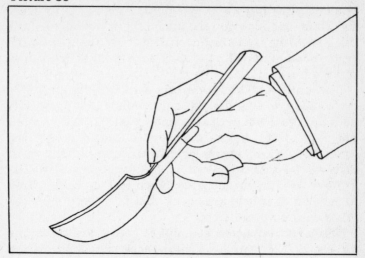

Correct holding of fish knife.

Picture 32 and move a portion of the meat or fish from the platter to your plate. If you're not sure of yourself, move as small a portion as you can. The smaller the portion, the easier it is to move.

Although the fork is often put underneath the fish or meat to transport it, if the meat or fish is covered by sauce or is juicy by nature, put the spoon underneath and encourage the person serving you to move the platter closer to you to avoid splatters. Return the serving utensils to the serving plate as indicated in Picture 33.

Vegetables should be placed on your plate in a neat, orderly manner. The person serving vegetables may come to you from either side and you should use a spoon with your right hand and a fork with the left. Again, keep your portions small. If the person who is serving you stands too far away, encourage him to move closer, particularly if you are not sure of what you're doing.

The standard American way of handling a knife and fork is to start with the fork in the left hand, prongs down. Use the fork to spear meat, fish, and vegetables so that you may hold them in a steady position while you cut with your knife. When you finish cutting, place the knife diagonally on the upper right-hand area of the plate with the blade facing in and move the fork to the right hand. Eat with the fork in the right hand, the prongs up.

The continental style of eating, which is gaining more favor today, is a far simpler method in which the fork is kept prongs down in the left hand, and the knife is used not only to cut, but to push and shove food onto the fork. The fork is always held in the manner shown in Pictures 34 and 35, never in any other manner. The knife is used to cut meat as shown in Picture 34. Used to cut fish, it is held always as shown in Picture 36. All other variations are incorrect.

Naturally, public or semipublic meals are occasions for social intercourse. During these occasions we are not expected simply to sit, stuff our faces, and leave. Therefore, you must know that when your hostess sets up a seating arrangement such as man/woman, man/woman, she expects the man to turn directly to the woman on his right and start talking. You are certainly not forbidden to talk to the person on your left, but you should be careful not to isolate the woman on your right. It is your social obligation to speak to her unless she is otherwise engaged.

The standard rules for good manners apply at the table as well as everywhere else. Never speak too loudly. You should not be heard by people at both ends of the table. The dinner table is not a lectern and you're not there to give a public speech. You must carry on polite, intimate conversation with the people seated nearby. Naturally, you don't chew with your mouth open or try to eat and talk at the same time.

When you are conversing, you're expected to put the knife and fork on your plate in the manner shown in Picture 37 which indicates that they are in a rest position. Note that the sharp edge of the knife is always pointed toward you and the fork is always placed prongs down. When you are finished, however, you place your knife and fork, again with the blade pointed in and the fork prongs down, in the position shown in Picture 39. This time they are parallel to each other. When you no longer require the fork, leave it on the plate as shown in Picture 38, prongs up. If the meal did not require the use of one of the implements that had been set out, leave that utensil on the table. Do not put it on the plate with the utensils you did use.

The rules for finger foods, which ones are and which aren't and how to deal with them, are very confused and vary from one section of the country to another. For example in the South, although table manners are far more important than they are in the North, there is a great deal more leeway as to which foods are finger foods. While in the North you may pick up such things as asparagus, bacon, the legs of small birds, cakes, celery, olives, and chicken at barbecues with your fingers and be reasonably sure of being correct, the South has a much more sensible rule: if it looks as though you can eat it neatly with your fingers, go right ahead. In the North, if you're not certain, eat the food with a knife and fork to be on the safe side. Asparagus, when it's too long or covered with hollandaise sauce, should be cut with a knife and fork. Cakes, caviar, fish, crepes, and any of the standard meats and vegetables require that you follow the rule of common sense.

Obviously, ice cream has to be eaten with a spoon unless it is so well frozen you can eat it along with your cake. Neatness is the goal. Although you can pick up a sandwich with both hands, it is generally considered more tasteful to cut it in halves or quarters and pick up one piece at a time.

There are a few details that you should keep in mind at all times. Never take anything from a serving plate directly into your mouth, including celery, olives, pickles, and such. Move celery and olives to your butter plate, salt them there, and then eat them. Never do two things at once, such as picking up a water glass to drink

Picture 37

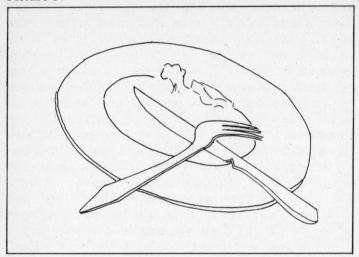

At rest position, knife and fork.

while unfolding your napkin with the other hand. It's always simplest to stop one action before starting another. When you start doing two things at the same time, you're liable to spill something or poke someone.

Common sense also extends to taking things from your mouth as well as putting things in. When you're eating grapes or watermelon, very small seeds can be deposited in the cupped hand. When eating large fruits such as peaches, cherries, and plums, good table manners require you to deposit the pits onto a spoon or fork and move them to your plate in that manner.

Finally, if you're going to eat spaghetti or lobster you should know that each requires particular skills. For spaghetti, twirl it on a fork against a large spoon. Lobster requires that you be deft with a shell cracker and that you eat various sections with your fingers, others with a fork and knife.

When I asked the men who run corporate America why they thought people made mistakes at the dinner table, they surprised me. Most of them said it wasn't

Picture 38

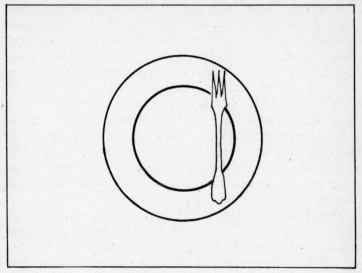

Finished position, fork alone.

Picture 39

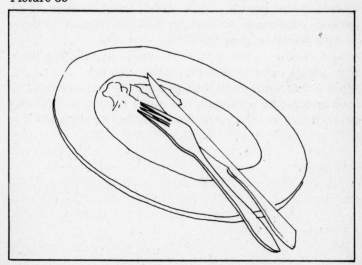

Finished position, knife and fork.

that people didn't know what to do. Subordinates often started correctly. They sat down, picked up their napkin, and put it on their lap, carried on polite conversation, and usually got through the first two or three courses successfully. But once the meal got going and they started feeling comfortable, they fell into their normal eating habits and started eating with their mouths open. If you're used to eating in front of television or with a plastic fork, you're going to find it very difficult to conduct yourself properly at a formal dinner. Again, I would suggest that at least two meals a weak be served at home in a very formal manner, if not for your sake, at least for your children's, so that they will have these essential skills as part of their baggage when they enter the outer world where it counts so much.

For those who need them, here is a simple list of don'ts. Don't hold your knife or fork in an improper manner. Don't eat with your mouth open. Don't leave a spoon in your cup or utensils in the dessert dish at the end of the meal; place them on the service dish. Don't put too much in your mouth at once. Don't talk with food in your mouth. Don't slouch in your seat, rock back in your chair, or apologize if you happen to burp or drop something on the floor.

And finally, when you're finished, don't push your plate away, open your vest, loosen your belt, and belch. Simply wait until your hostess has indicated the meal is over and get up when she has given the signal that she is about to leave the table. Never before. Bon Appetit!

14

PRACTICE FOR SUCCESS

The last chapter in most books announces the beginning of the end; in this book it announces only the beginning. As I told you earlier, I have no formula for easy, instant success, and therefore I think it's inappropriate to end this book with the traditional pep talk that closes most success books. Instead, I am going to invite you to "live for success," to take a realistic look at yourself and to spend weeks, months, possibly even years mastering social, business and personal skills, all of which will increase your chance to succeed in anything you do.

Having given success courses to thousands of men and women, I understand that readers at this point will fall into six basic groups.

Type One, the self-starting perfectionists, have already analyzed their shortcomings, outlined a realistic plan for overcoming them, and have probably begun practicing before reaching this part of the book. If you are one of them, you may not have specific goals and a timetable in your mind at this moment but you will develop them almost by instinct. You are the people who are most likely to succeed. Frankly, you don't need this chapter, but, being Type One, you won't be able to resist reading it. You complete everything you start and you invariably do it well. Obviously, all I can do is wish you luck.

The Type Twos are procrastinators. Their favorite saying is "Not now, I'll get to it later." They really intend to do something about what they've read, they just can't get around to it this week. They hope they may be able to get to it next week or next month but are not quite sure. We know they'll never really get around to it unless we give them a shove and a schedule. I know how procrastinators think. They have a million excuses. Forget them! The trick is to make a definite commitment to start *now, not tomorrow.*

Next we come to the Type Threes, who represent the majority of readers. Their road to hell will be paved with good intentions. They have spotted one or two shortcomings and they are determined to overcome them but their problem is they have no sense of organization or the self-discipline that comes with it. They never bother to figure out exactly what they're going to do. Their plans are too general. They never have a program and therefore they very seldom accomplish much. It is the main reason for their failure. They will find themselves squaring their shoulders and standing a bit more erect for the next few days. They may even begin to listen a bit more carefully to how they speak. But unless they set up a definite program, with a specific set of goals, this book will have little effect on their lives. If you are one of them—and most readers are—I suggest you put the book down now and get a pen, because you're the type who must commit to writing everything you're going to do. The existence of a written document, a black-and-white schedule, acts as an army sergeant. It drills you. You're the typical middle-class soldier: you don't *join* the army but if you're drafted you fight like hell. In the war against failure you must draft yourself.

Type Fours are the professional success-seekers. They read every book with success in the title but they never seem to succeed. They read this book and they weigh it no more heavily than the books written by a million idiots. They're out to get simple success, instant success, and downhill success. They want that secret no one has told them yet and they far prefer authors who promise it to them. The fact that these authors don't deliver doesn't bother them too much. If you are one of these people, I'm going to disappoint you. The one characteristic of people who are successful is they don't believe in instant success. If you believe in instant success, you'll probably never succeed. You must sit down, take a deep breath, and say, "In order to succeed I have to sweat, I have to work, I have to plan, and there's no time like the present to start."

Then, there is the group for whom I have the most sympathy: the Fives. They are overwhelmed by an enormous amount of information. They see so many flaws in themselves, they don't know where to start. They're frankly discouraged by the task that confronts them. This group will find this chapter particularly useful. I will help you set up priorities, goals, and realistic timetables for achieving them and, by doing so, eliminate that sense of being overwhelmed. You can succeed if you try and have a plan.

Finally, there are the Sixes. They are the people who are already successful or well on their way to success, who come to my meetings, read my research reports and buy my books. Their usual comments about my work is, "Of course, of course, oh that's an interesting point." Coming to a success seminar for them is a busman's holiday. They are like opera buffs going to an opera lecture—they may know more than the lecturer, but they come anyway because they enjoy the subject. I am flattered and sometimes astounded by their presence and can state without any hesitation that this chapter is not necessary for them because they run America. They don't need John T. Molloy.

The first step in success training is to identify those areas that need improvement. Most of the time this is

simple. You know whether you are unpopular or unable
to give orders and we've given you a fair idea of whether
you are operating correctly as an office politician or a
corporate wife. Most of you will have no trouble listing
a half dozen areas in which you would like to improve
and listing them in order of importance. Doing so here
is the first step in goal setting.

1.

2.

3.

4.

5.

6.

If you had difficulty choosing which areas need
improvement or which areas you should work on first,
I've developed a little form that may help. The areas in
the form are communications skills, power skills, body
signals, verbal signals, popularity skills, interview skills,
and sales skills. These areas correspond to chapter head-
ings, but you may, of course, substitute any of your
own. I've also listed more precise areas of study. If you
decide you need to work on power language, or improve
your body signals specifically for interviews, you should
certainly do so. Finally, I've listed Dressing for Success,
which is the subject of my earlier books. There are
recognized success skills which are not covered in this
book or may be peculiar to a particular industry or
geographical location. If you decide you need to work
on a social or business skill not included in the chart, do
so. It should be part of your personal success-program.
Please note that I've left three empty spaces for you to
fill in anything you wish. Also, feel free to cross out any

of the sections we've filled in—they are simply guides—
and replace them with your own improvement goals.

The following chart rates each of the areas for improvement on a one-to-ten basis with ten being the highest
score.

If you don't have a good reason for rearranging them,
I suggest you attack one area at a time and start with
the area with the highest score. Since you are your own
teacher, I advise you to rig the course and give yourself
an "A." One of the easiest ways to get students interested is to let them start in an area in which they've
already had some success, in which they're not going to
have too much difficulty and in which their accomplishments will produce an immediate reward. Our experience shows that nothing succeeds like success. When
our students succeed in one area, they quickly go on to
a second and a third area and do just as well.

AREAS FOR IMPROVEMENT	PRESENT ABILITY	EASE OF ACCOM- PLISH- MENT	ESTIMATED IMPACT WITHIN 1 YEAR	TOTALS
1. Communi- cations				
2. Power Skills				
3. Body Signals				
4. Verbal Messages				
5. Popularity Skills				
6. Interview Skills				
7. Sales Skills				
8. Body Signals for Interviews				

AREAS FOR IMPROVEMENT	PRESENT ABILITY	EASE OF ACCOM- PLISH- MENT	ESTIMATED IMPACT WITHIN 1 YEAR	TOTALS
9. Power Language				
10.				
11.				
12.				

Naturally, the first rule you should apply to any area, including self-improvement, is common sense. If you're presently out of work, or if you're working and looking for a job, it would be silly for you to undertake a major study of communication skills. It would be far more sensible for you to master the interview chapter and overcome shortcomings you have in that area. Obviously, the same is true if you are an executive wife. Although you might be far more interested in developing your power skills than your social skills, it would seem that those social skills that were connected with being an executive wife would be the most sensible projects to undertake first. Being sensible is not enough. You must commit yourself to action. You must choose those areas you wish to improve and the ones you're going to work on immediately.

Areas for Improvement

1.

2.

3.

4.

5.

6.

Now that you have six areas listed in the order in which you are going to attack them, you may find it more efficient to divide some of them into subsections. If you've chosen table manners as your first area, I do not think subsections are necessary. You simply have to memorize the uses of various utensils and practice with them. If, however, you choose to develop your power skills, you will have to decide how much time and effort you're going to give visual power signals, verbal power signals, or power language. You will have to practice each power element independently and then practice them together with either the aid of your family or a mechanical device.

After you've divided your areas of study into subsections, you have to develop a plan of attack. First, write down what you hope to accomplish. Be as specific as possible. We found in our success courses that once students committed themselves to a goal in writing, they felt obliged to reach it. When goals were not put down in black and white, students tended to lower their sights and this became self-defeating. Most of us, unfortunately, are basically lazy and we seek the path of least resistance, if that path is left open. Writing down your goals and being specific closes the path of least resistance and forces you to keep your sights high.

Next you must set up a schedule for reaching goals. Before attempting to do this you have to analyze the type of learning involved in reaching different skills. There are three types. First there are informational skills. If before reading this book you were not able to identify a fish knife and now you can, you have an informational skill. If you are served a fish course you will now be able to choose the right utensil. The second type of learning has to do with use of a fish knife. The fact that you know how to hold a fish knife will do you little good without practice. And, finally, there is habitual knowledge. If you've only used meat knives, it will take practice before you use a fish knife correctly. Habitual knowledge is really the only kind that will give you the self-assurance you need to handle the fish course and conversation with the lady next to you at a formal banquet.

Most of the so-called success books that I've read imply that if you possess information, you automatically have a foot up on the ladder of success. Once you've read those books, you're saved from a life of failure and destined for success. This is just not so. My research shows that information alone is useful in only a small percentage of cases. In most real-life situations, knowledge must become habit before it is truly useful.

If you've read carefully, you know a great deal about success and you have at your fingertips a basis for making judgments. The fact that we know that men from upper-middle-class backgrounds carry their shoulders differently from men from a lower-middle-class background and women from an upper-middle-class background hold their heads differently from women from a lower-middle-class background will be of very little use to you unless you act on the information. If you come from a blue-collar background, you're going to have to practice sitting or standing with your shoulders back or your head erect. My experience in teaching success courses has shown that it would be best if you set up a specific time of day for practicing sitting and standing. I know this may sound silly to people who've never tried it, because their instinct is to say, "I'll do it all the time; everytime it occurs to me I'll stand up straight." But experience shows if you set aside as little as fifteen minutes a day for posture practice your improvement will be two or three times greater than if you spend twenty-four hours a day without a schedule. In addition, sitting every night before a television set will give you a way of measuring your progress. The first night you sit erect for fifteen minutes, you'll be very uncomfortable, but after six or seven weeks you'll be able to sit erect for fifteen minutes and enjoy the television program without even realizing you're doing it.

Now I know there are some of you who want to go one

step farther and set up a six-week course in body language and a three-week course in verbal skills and a four-week course in social skills, but that is really not possible. What you must do is work until you perfect it. There are no C's in success, only A's.

Success does not mean that you cannot fail, it means you cannot accept failure.

LEARN TO SPEAK CORRECTLY AT HOME IN YOUR SPARE TIME

If, after reading *Live for Success*, you come to the conclusion that you and/or members of your family, particularly your children, need improved verbal patterns, we have very good news for you.

Dr. William Formaad, in addition to being one of the leaders in this field, the head of the speech department of a major university, and the man executives seek when one of their number needs help, has developed a unique method of speech training that is designed to help you self-evaluate, self-motivate, and self-correct your speech patterns. The entire course consists of five forty-minute cassette tapes which you will play over and over as you experiment, practice, and improve this essential image skill. These lessons emphasize crispness and articulation, clarity and projection of tone, esthetic appeal and a reasonable conformity to cultivated usage. The object of this course is to help you develop the speech patterns of well-educated men and women from privileged backgrounds, which is the pattern of successful speech in America.

Mr. John T. Molloy
P.O. Box 526
Washington Bridge Station
New York, N.Y. 10033

Please send me Dr. Formaad's Live for Success Speech Course. Enclosed is my check for $80.00 to cover the complete cost of the program. Outside U.S. add $3.00.

Name_____

Address_____

_____

If you need help choosing proper success clothing, you may in addition use this form to order John T. Molloy's "Dress for Success Computer Printout." Check the appropriate box.   Male ☐   Female ☐   And enclose a check for $24.95 for each program.

ABOUT THE AUTHOR

JOHN T. MOLLOY'S two earlier books—*Dress for Success* and *The Woman's Dress for Success Book*—have sold over two million copies and have literally changed the look of corporate America.

These books, along with Molloy's research techniques, are taught in hundreds of universities both here and abroad. He has also been a consultant to over 380 of the *Fortune* 500, to scores of the largest companies in Europe and Japan, and to dozens of governments.